T0289644

Happiness and Wellbeing in Singapore

To present a multifaceted and holistic perspective of what makes Singaporeans happy, Tambyah, Tan and Yuen discuss the findings and insights from the 2022 Quality of Life Survey, which examines the perceptions and views of 1,905 Singapore citizens. This is the latest survey in a series of studies on the wellbeing of Singaporeans.

While the impact of the COVID-19 pandemic on wellbeing is a timely discussion, the findings are also compared with previous surveys conducted in 2011 and 2016 to provide a longitudinal perspective of how Singaporeans' wellbeing has evolved over the years. Key aspects of this topic include life satisfaction and satisfaction with specific life domains, aspects of affective wellbeing (e.g., happiness, enjoyment and achievement), economic wellbeing, psychological flourishing, personal values, value orientations and views on socio-political issues. Pertinent differences due to demographics such as gender, marital status, age, education and household income are also highlighted. The book also features four archetypes and clusters of Singaporeans, which are representative of the unique demographics, values and wellbeing outcomes examined.

The findings and insights will be useful to academics, policy makers, practitioners, students and the general public who are interested in understanding the life satisfaction and wellbeing of Singaporeans.

Siok Kuan Tambyah is an associate professor at the NUS Business School, National University of Singapore (NUS). Her research and teaching interests include consumption and identity, consumer culture, happiness and pedagogical research on residential colleges. She has published extensively, with her most recent publication being *Student Growth and Development in New Higher Education Learning Spaces; Student-Centred Learning in Singapore.*

Tan Soo Jiuan is an honorary fellow at the NUS Business School. She has published in leading international journals, and co-authored several books: *Understanding Singaporeans: Values, Lifestyles, Aspirations and Consumption Behaviors, Happiness and Wellbeing: The Singaporean Experience, Happiness, Wellbeing and Society: What Matters for Singaporeans,* and *Competing for Markets: Growth Strategies for SMEs.*

Yuen Wei Lun is a PhD student at the NUS Business School. He is particularly interested in exploring the psychological factors that influence human decision-making, with an emphasis on promoting sustainability, consumer wellbeing, and responsible consumption. As a budding researcher, his research has been published in the *Journal of Personality.*

Routledge Focus on Business and Management

The fields of business and management have grown exponentially as areas of research and education. This growth presents challenges for readers trying to keep up with the latest important insights. *Routledge Focus on Business and Management* presents small books on big topics and how they intersect with the world of business research.

Individually, each title in the series provides coverage of a key academic topic, whilst collectively, the series forms a comprehensive collection across the business disciplines.

Women's Social Entrepreneurship
Case Studies from the United Kingdom
Panagiotis Kyriakopoulos

Business Schools post-Covid-19
A Blueprint for Survival
Andreas Kaplan

Sustainable Governance in B Corps
Non-Financial Reporting for Sustainable Development
Patrizia Gazzola and Matteo Ferioli

Happiness and Wellbeing in Singapore
Beyond Economic Prosperity
Siok Kuan Tambyah, Tan Soo Jiuan and Yuen Wei Lun

For more information about this series, please visit: www.routledge.com/Routledge-Focus-on-Business-and-Management/book-series/FBM

Happiness and Wellbeing in Singapore

Beyond Economic Prosperity

**Siok Kuan Tambyah, Tan Soo Jiuan
and Yuen Wei Lun**

LONDON AND NEW YORK

First published 2024
by Routledge
4 Park Square, Milton Park, Abingdon, Oxon, OX14 4RN

and by Routledge
605 Third Avenue, New York, NY 10158

Routledge is an imprint of the Taylor & Francis Group, an informa business

British Library Cataloguing-in-Publication Data
A catalogue record for this book is available from the British Library

Library of Congress Cataloging-in-Publication Data
Names: Tambyah, Siok Kuan, author. |
Tan, Soo Jiuan, author. | Yuen, WeiLun, author.
Title: Happiness and wellbeing in Singapore : beyond economic prosperity /
Siok Kuan Tambyah, Tan Soo Jiuan and Yuen Wei Lun.
Description: Abingdon, Oxon ; New York, NY : Routledge, 2024. |
Series: Routledge focus on business and management |
Includes bibliographical references and index. |
Identifiers: LCCN 2023026728 (print) | LCCN 2023026729 (ebook) |
ISBN 9781032507873 (hardback) | ISBN 9781032507880 (paperback) |
ISBN 9781003399650 (ebook)
Subjects: LCSH: Quality of life–Singapore–Statistics. |
Singapore–Social conditions–Statistics.
Classification: LCC HN700.67.A85 T356 2024 (print) |
LCC HN700.67.A85 (ebook) | DDC 306.095957–dc23/eng/20230626
LC record available at https://lccn.loc.gov/2023026728
LC ebook record available at https://lccn.loc.gov/2023026729

ISBN: 9781032507873 (hbk)
ISBN: 9781032507880 (pbk)
ISBN: 9781003399650 (ebk)

DOI: 10.4324/9781003399650

Typeset in Times New Roman
by Newgen Publishing UK

The Open Access version of this book was funded by National University of
Singapore.

To my father, Khoo Tian Lock, who taught and showed me how to live a happy and meaningful life. – *Siok Kuan Tambyah*

To my mother, Lim Yam Peng, who is a great role model for me, but a tough act to follow. – *Tan Soo Jiuan*

To my wife, Delphinna, who is my constant source of support and inspiration, and to my "dogter", Nugget, who probably can't read this. – *Yuen Wei Lun*

Contents

Figures

Tables

More about the authors

Siok Kuan Tambyah is an associate professor at the NUS Business School, National University of Singapore (NUS), and a fellow at the College of Alice & Peter Tan at NUS. Her research and teaching interests include consumption and identity, consumer culture, happiness and cross-cultural consumer behavior. She has taught and published extensively in these areas and has co-authored four books on happiness research. In addition to disciplinary research, she is involved in pedagogical research on the learning processes and outcomes in residential colleges. Her most recent publication is *Student Growth and Development in New Higher Education Learning Spaces: Student-Centred Learning in Singapore.*

Tan Soo Jiuan is an honorary fellow at the NUS Business School. Her research and teaching interests are in the areas of international market entry strategies, consumer values and lifestyles, parallel importing, game theoretic applications in marketing and product and brand management. She has published in leading international journals such as *Journal of Business Ethics, Journal of International Business Studies, Social Indicators Research* and *Marketing Letters,* and is also the co-author of six books: *Seven Faces of Singaporeans, Competing for Markets: Growth Strategies for SMEs, Understanding Singaporeans: Values, Lifestyles, Aspirations and Consumption Behaviors, The Wellbeing of Singaporeans, Happiness and Wellbeing: The Singaporean Experience* and *Happiness, Wellbeing and Society: What Matters for Singaporeans.*

Yuen Wei Lun is a PhD student at the NUS Business School. He is particularly interested in exploring the psychological factors that influence human decision-making, with an emphasis on promoting sustainability, consumer wellbeing and responsible consumption. As a budding researcher, his research has been published in the *Journal of Personality*.

Acknowledgements

We would like to express our appreciation to Keith Chua for his interest in and support for quality of life research, and the Mrs Lee Choon Guan Trust Fund for their generous funding for the 2022 QOL Survey. We would like to thank the 1,905 Singaporeans whose perceptions of happiness and wellbeing are represented and analyzed in this survey. We would also like to acknowledge the research support provided by the National University of Singapore in terms of the Qualtrics license and ethics approval.

In the preparation of this book, we are extremely grateful for the contributions of:

(1) Nicole Ariana Lim Shankar, who diligently updated the literature and statistics for Chapters 1 and 4;
(2) Carmen Yow Jia Wen, an exceptional honors student in political science, who updated the literature and provided insights for Chapters 7 and 8, and also put in many hours of work for copy-editing; and
(3) our co-author Yuen Wei Lun for his perseverance in data analyses and his creativity in presenting the results in formats that greatly facilitate one's reading and comprehension of the survey findings.

1 Introduction, context and research methodology

This book focuses on the wellbeing of Singaporeans and details the findings of the 2022 Quality of Life (QOL) Survey, a large-scale survey of 1,905 citizens conducted from June 2022 to July 2022. This comprehensive study provides insights into Singaporeans' satisfaction with life and various life domains, happiness, enjoyment, achievement, control, purpose, psychological flourishing, economic wellbeing, personal values, value orientations, views about democratic rights and politics and what they experienced during the COVID-19 pandemic. The 2022 QOL Survey also examines the impact of the COVID-19 pandemic on the wellbeing of Singaporeans. To provide a longitudinal perspective into how the various aspects of this topic have evolved through the years, we compare the findings of this current QOL Survey with the most recent ones conducted in 2011 and 2016.

In the sections to follow, we first provide some background information relating to Singapore's demographic, economic, and political development. This provides readers, both new to and familiar with Singapore, some insights into the context in which the survey was conducted. The 2019, 2020, 2021 and 2022 statistics were retrieved from various websites and databases as noted in the references. We then discuss our rationale for conducting the QOL Surveys in Singapore, considering the sustained interest in wellbeing research in many parts of the world. Finally, we outline the research methodology for the 2022 QOL Survey, including the questionnaire development, sampling procedures, data quality control, the profile of respondents, the representativeness of the sample and data analyses.

DOI: 10.4324/9781003399650-1

Demographics and human development

Singapore is a multi-ethnic, multi-religious and multi-lingual society. At the end of June 2022, according to the Singapore Department of Statistics website, the resident population of Singaporeans and Permanent Residents consisted of Chinese as the dominant ethnic group (74.1 per cent), followed by Malays (13.6 per cent), Indians (9.0 per cent) and Others (3.2 per cent) (Department of Statistics Singapore, 2022a). There is considerable freedom and plurality in the practice of religions such as Buddhism, Christianity, Islam, Hinduism, and more. The national language is Malay, but the other official languages of English, Mandarin and Tamil are widely spoken by the population (Department of Statistics Singapore, 2022b).

As at end June 2022, the population in Singapore was estimated to be 5.64 million, of which 4.07 million were residents. Based on 2022 figures from the Singapore Department of Statistics' (DOS) website, the life expectancy at birth of Singapore residents was 83.5 years in 2021 (a decrease of 0.2 years compared with 83.7 years in 2019 before the COVID-19 pandemic), with males averaging 81.1 years and females 85.9 years (Department of Statistics Singapore, 2022c). Among residents aged 25 years and over, 61.8 per cent have obtained at least a postsecondary school education. This was mainly due to the increase in university graduates, from 24.5 per cent to 36.1 per cent over the decade from 2011 to 2021.

The Human Development Index (HDI) looks at happiness not just from an economic perspective but also including health and education. The index comprises three components: national income, life expectancy and literacy. It classifies countries into one of three clusters according to their attainment of human development. Among the 191 countries in the 2021–2022 HDI Report, Singapore was ranked 12th with a score of 0.939 (United Nations Development Programme, 2023). Singapore is in the very high development cluster and more highly ranked than Japan (19th) and South Korea (20th) but behind Hong Kong (4th). Singapore usually has a strong showing on the HDI because of its strong economic performance (GDP) and the favorable statistics about life expectancy and literacy.

Economic development, governance and stability

Since its independence in 1965, the People's Action Party has been predominantly the ruling political party. This political stability, coupled with a largely effective government and administration, have contributed to Singapore's economic development which is primarily based on a market-driven system. According to the Singapore Department of Statistics and figures released in 2022, Singapore's GDP for 2022 was S$643,546 million (Department of Statistics Singapore, 2022d). The economy grew at 3.6 per cent and the per capita GDP was reported to be S$114,165. According to the 2022 Key Household Income Trends, among resident employed households, the median monthly household income from work grew by 6.1 per cent in nominal terms, from $9,520 in 2021 to $10,099 in 2022 (Department of Statistics Singapore, 2022e). After adjusting for inflation, the median monthly household income from work rose 0.2 per cent in real terms in 2022. Inflation has seen a sharp increase from 2.31 per cent in 2021 (O'Neill, 2022) to 6.1 per cent in 2022 (Huang, 2023). Nevertheless, there was an improvement in the unemployment rate. Compared to 2021, which saw an overall unemployment rate of 2.7 per cent, figures stood at 2.1 per cent in 2022, a figure that was lower than the prepandemic level (Ministry of Manpower Singapore, 2023). The Ministry of Manpower noted that over the last 10 years, from 2012 to 2022, the average number of paid hours worked per week remained relatively constant, at around 45 to 46 hours.

In the 2022 Index of Economic Freedom published by the Heritage Foundation, which ranks 177 nations in terms of their levels of economic freedom, Singapore was assessed as 84.4 per cent free, making it the world's freest economy (The Heritage Foundation, 2022a). The assessment of economic freedom was based on 12 measures along four dimensions as follows: rule of law, government size, regulatory efficiency and open markets. Singapore performed well in trade freedom (95.0), property rights (94.4), government integrity (92.8) and tax burden (90.5) (The Heritage Foundation, 2022b).

According to surveys examined by Transparency International and the Corruption Perceptions Index that they computed, Singapore was perceived to have the least corrupt public sector among Asian nations in 2021 (Transparency International, 2021), and was also ranked at 4th (6th in 2017) on a global scale of 180 countries with a score of 8.5 (8.4 in 2017) (Transparency International, 2017). The countries ranked ahead of Singapore were New Zealand, Finland and Denmark (joint 1st). Countries such as Sweden and Norway ranked 4th with Singapore as well. The 2021 report on Corruption in Asia by Political and Economic Risk Consultancy (PERC) Ltd. rated Singapore's government as having the highest level of integrity in Asia, Australia and the United States (Corrupt Practices Investigation Bureau, 2021). Its level of corruption had a score of 1.68, followed by Australia (2.15), Japan (2.75), Hong Kong (3.95) and Macau (4.85).

Political rights and civil liberties

Although Singapore is ranked highly in terms of economic freedom, political freedom is less favorably assessed. The Freedom in the World is a global annual report, published by international nongovernmental organization Freedom House, that assesses the real-world rights and freedoms enjoyed by individuals, rather than the performance of the state. Measuring scores and status, each country is awarded zero to four points for 25 indicators, with the maximum score of 100 points. These indicators are grouped into categories of political rights (0–40) and civil liberties (0–60) (Freedom House, 2022a). These scores are weighted equally to determine whether the country or territory's status is "free", "partly free", or "not free". In the 2022 report, Singapore maintained its "partly free" status, attaining a score of 28 for civil liberties and 19 for political rights (Freedom House, 2022b).

Social progress

The Social Progress Index determines what it means to be a good society according to three dimensions: basic human needs (nutrition and basic medical care, water and sanitation, shelter, and personal safety); foundations of wellbeing (basic knowledge, information and communications, health and wellness, and environmental quality); and opportunity (personal rights, personal freedom and choice, inclusiveness, and access to advanced education) (Social

Progress Imperative, 2021). These 12 components form the Social Progress framework. With a GDP PPP per capita of $93,397 (2nd out of 163 countries), Singapore had a score of 84.73 out of 100 on the 2022 Social Progress Index (30th out of 168 countries) (Social Progress Imperative, 2022). Singapore's scorecard indicated that it ranked 2nd out of 163 countries for GDP PPP per capita. For the overall basic human needs dimension, Singapore ranked 3rd. Under the basic human needs dimension, Singapore was also ranked 3rd for shelter and 2nd for personal safety. For foundations of wellbeing, Singapore also ranked 4th for health and wellness.

Rationale for the QOL Surveys in Singapore

Research on wellbeing has been ongoing for many years around the world. Many varied concerns ranging from the economics of happiness to the eudemonics of happiness have been addressed in academic circles, as well as in the policy-making arena. Researchers involved in wellbeing research have noted the limitations in using GNP and GDP as a measurement for or indicator of the quality of life because there are other aspects of wellbeing that cannot be accounted for with economic prosperity. We also recognize these limitations in a relatively wealthy country like Singapore, and the need for a more holistic perspective of wellbeing.

As recommended in the report by the Commission on the Measurement of Economic Performance and Social Progress, "measures of subjective wellbeing provide key information about people's quality of life. Statistical offices should incorporate questions to capture people's life evaluations, hedonic experiences and priorities in their own surveys" (Stiglitz et al., 2009, p.58). Currently, there are many well-regarded worldwide surveys and indices administered by various national agencies and governments, international agencies (e.g., the Organization for Economic Co-operation and Development [OECD], United Nations, etc.) and research institutes. Singapore has been a part of some worldwide surveys, notably, the Gallup World Poll and the World Values Survey.

Many countries and regions have their own versions of a quality-of-life (QOL) and wellbeing survey that is focused on their particularistic needs and contexts (e.g., the European Social Survey). Bhutan even instituted its own happiness index with unique indicators such as community vitality, cultural diversity and resilience, time use and ecological diversity and resilience (GNH Centre Bhutan, n.d.). Some of these surveys and indices are administered by government agencies, while others are from independently founded research agencies. For the Singaporean context, we have tried to collect data on the wellbeing of Singaporeans every five years since 1996. These QOL Surveys incorporate validated measures used in other research studies (for comparison across countries) and context-specific measures (for comparison across years within Singapore). The datasets for the QOL Surveys provide the indicators of wellbeing that are relevant to Singaporeans for more in-depth analyses.

Research methodology

Both objective and subjective indicators are needed for a meaningful assessment of the QOL of Singaporeans. Many objective indicators are available from the Singapore Department of Statistics. Thus, the nationwide 2022 QOL Survey (like its predecessors) focuses on subjective indicators (evaluations and perceptions). We also collect information on the demographic background of the respondents. These research endeavors are premised on a robust research methodology that yields a credible and representative sample. This, in turn, enables comprehensive data analyses to be carried out with comparisons to data sets from previous QOL Surveys in 2011 and 2016.

Questionnaire development

Based on a review of recent research on wellbeing, and feedback from the 2011 and 2016 QOL Surveys, we discussed what to include in the 2022 QOL Survey. For instance, questions on the impact of the COVID-19 pandemic were adapted from the Institute of Policy Studies' (IPS) working paper on the impact of COVID-19 on Singaporeans (Mathews et al., 2021) and the World Happiness Report (Helliwell et al., 2021). To facilitate longitudinal comparisons, most of the key items relating to satisfaction with various aspects of life, and the value orientations examined in the 2011 and 2016 QOL Surveys were retained for the 2022 QOL Survey.

Like its predecessors, the 2022 QOL Survey questionnaire was first drafted in English and pretested among a small group of potential respondents. Any ambiguities or inconsistencies were eliminated based on the feedback collected. The survey questionnaire was then translated into Chinese, Malay and Tamil for respondents who were not familiar with English. This was completed by the market research firm that was tasked to conduct the fieldwork.

The 2022 QOL Survey questionnaire consisted of 145 questions in 11 sections. Generally, the survey questionnaire was comprehensive and covered many aspects of the quality of life of the respondents. For this book, we have selected a list of variables for in-depth analyses, as shown in Table 1.1. The main outcome variables or wellbeing outcomes include satisfaction with life, happiness, enjoyment, achievement, control and purpose. In Chapter 4, we also included a measure on satisfaction with the overall QOL. The main input variables are questions related to personal values, value orientations, views about democratic rights and politics and the impact of the COVID-19 pandemic. More details of the measures and scale items will be shared in the respective chapters with the data analyses and the results.

Sampling frame

The study covered a nationally representative sample of the general population in Singapore aged 21 to 79 years old. It was launched on 23 June 2022 and closed on 25 July 2022 using Qualtrics (www.qualtrics.com), an online survey platform. Data collection was done through online means for the 2022 QOL Survey, as there was uncertainty about whether door-to-door data collection would be allowed due to safe distancing restrictions. Even if this was possible, the timeliness and efficiency would be adversely affected due to additional precautions during the COVID-19 pandemic. To ensure that good-quality data and a representative sample would still be obtained, we worked closely with Qualtrics to ensure that the sampling procedures were robust, and safeguards for data quality control were in place. As a panel aggregator, Qualtrics works with online sample partners to supply the respondents needed for this

Table 1.1 Overview of input variables, output variables and demographics

Main Input Variables	Value Orientations	Family Values, Sustainability, Traditionalism and Materialism
	Personal Values (List of Values)	Sense of belonging, excitement, fun and enjoyment in life, warm relationships with others, self-fulfilment, being well-respected, sense of accomplishment, security and self-respect
Additional Input Variables	Generalized Trust	Whether people can be trusted, and would they try to be fair and helpful?
	Trust in post-pandemic times	Trust in the government and fellow citizens to navigate the postpandemic world
	Satisfaction with democratic rights, and views about politics	Right to vote, to participate in any form of organization, to gather and demonstrate, to be informed about the work and functions of government, freedom of speech and to criticize the government
	Impact of the COVID-19 pandemic	Economic impact, health risks, familial factors and social disruptions
Input/ Control Variables	Demographics	Of the respondent, and the household the respondent lives in.
		Gender, marital status, age, education and monthly household income
Output Variables	Wellbeing outcomes (cognitive aspects)	Satisfaction with life, satisfaction with 15 life domains
		Satisfaction with the overall QOL in general
		Life evaluations using the Cantril Ladder
	Wellbeing outcomes (affective aspects)	Happiness, enjoyment, achievement, control, purpose, psychological flourishing
	Additional wellbeing outcomes	Economic wellbeing

study. All eligible respondents provided informed consent via electronic means. The survey was administered anonymously with no personally identifiable information.

Sampling method

Step 1: Choosing sample partner

When choosing the sample partners, Qualtrics leverages multiple sources to best fit the client's needs. Sample partners are selected on a project-by-project basis and are chosen based on the project's specific requirements and Qualtrics's past experience or engagement with the sample partners. Also, we ensured that all sample partners employed continuous monitoring and quality control checks.

The majority of sample sources provided by the sample partners come from traditional, actively managed, double-opt-in market research panels. This is also the preferred method in the industry. To ensure profiles of respondents in these sample sources are consistently updated, Qualtrics's network of sample partners requests updates for profiling questions at various cadences. In general, the questions asked across sample sources are similar, with some variations for more specific profiling questions.

Step 2: Sample deployment

Once the sample partners have been selected, the sample deployment process involves sending survey invites to the respondents in the panels. For this study, potential respondents were sent an invitation informing them that a survey which matched their profile was available. Notifications in various forms (e.g., mail, in-app, email) were sent to the respondents, and rounds of follow-up reminders were also sent. Basic information such as the research purpose, the duration or time required to take the survey, the incentives to be received on completing the survey, information on confidentiality and a link to the privacy policy was shared with the respondents via email. To avoid biases, survey invitations do not include specific details about the contents.

For this study, the sample partners of Qualtrics randomly selected eligible respondents with the aim of national representation through routers and sophisticated Application Programming

Interface (API). To enhance the representativeness of the sample, Qualtrics used a simple random sampling strategy to recruit potential respondents by matching population demographics to the survey. When Qualtrics leverages a router from one of the sample partners, the sample partner directs panelists by matching the qualifying demographic information from their profiles to a specific survey. Sometimes, additional questions are asked prior to survey entry to ensure qualification. All processes related to the routers are randomized to avoid source bias. The routers that Qualtrics leverages are randomized, though sometimes with study prioritization or weighting. However, randomization requirements are always prioritized and protected. Sample partners are careful to prevent self-selection bias caused by invitation wording, survey topic or reward offerings.

Step 3: Incentivizing the respondents

On completion of the survey, respondents received an incentive based on the length of the survey, their specific panelist profile and target acquisition difficulty, among other factors. The specific type of rewards varies and may include cash, airline miles, gift cards, redeemable points, charitable donations, sweepstakes and vouchers.

Data quality control

To ensure that good-quality data is collected, "data scrubbing" was performed by Qualtrics after receiving all the survey responses to remove unfavorable data in order to optimize data accuracy and reliability. Data scrubbing refers to the procedure of recoding or removing incorrect, inaccurately formatted or repeated data in a database. The key objective of data scrubbing is to make the data accurate and consistent for analysis. Data scrubbing is used to identify survey responders that are not paying attention while taking the survey or taking the survey just for incentives (also known as professional responders).

We also checked to ensure respondents are coming from the country the survey is designed for. This is done via mapping IP address to the country. With the geolocation technique, Qualtrics ensured that the respondents taking the survey were Singapore citizens. When all the checks for data integrity and quality were finalized, Qualtrics provided the complete dataset and code book to the research team for data analyses.

The profile of respondents

The demographic backgrounds of the respondents in this study are presented in Table 1.2. As indicated, the gender balance was about equal (51 per cent male versus 49 per cent female). More

Table 1.2 Profile of respondents

2022 QOL Survey	N	Per cent
1. Gender		
- Male	972	51.0
- Female	933	49.0
Total	1905	100.0
2. Marital status		
- Single	778	40.8
- Married	1127	59.2
Total	1905	100.0
3. Age (years)		
- 21–24	167	8.8
- 25–29	252	13.2
- 30–34	283	14.9
- 35–39	196	10.3
- 40–44	257	13.5
- 45–49	208	10.9
- 50–54	203	10.7
- 55–59	141	7.4
- 60–64	117	6.1
- 65–69	47	2.5
- 70–74	20	1.0
- 75–79	14	0.7
Total	1905	100.0
4. Education		
- Primary school & below	21	1.1
- Secondary/ITE	302	15.9
- GCE A/Diploma	425	22.3
- University and above	1157	60.8
Total	1905	100.0

(Continued)

Table 1.2 (Continued)

2022 QOL Survey	N	Per cent
5. Household Income (monthly)		
- Less than $1,000	75	3.9
- $1,000–$1,999	66	3.5
- $2,000–$2,999	100	5.2
- $3,000–$3,999	136	7.1
- $4,000–$4,999	112	5.9
- $5,000–$5,999	120	6.3
- $6,000–$6,999	131	6.9
- $7,000–$7,999	135	7.1
- $8,000–$8,999	107	5.6
- $9,000–$9,999	117	6.1
- $10,000–$10,999	177	9.3
- $11,000–$11,999	80	4.2
- $12,000–$12,999	90	4.7
- $13,000–$13,999	78	4.1
- $14,000–$14,999	76	4.0
- $15,000–$17,499	96	5.0
- $17,500–$19,999	72	3.8
- $20,000 and above	137	7.2
Total	1905	100.0
6. Race		
- Chinese	1442	75.7
- Malay	288	15.1
- Indian	126	6.6
- Others	49	2.6
Total	1905	100.0

than half (59.2 per cent) of the respondents were married, and 95.8 per cent of the respondents were below 65 years of age. Chinese respondents accounted for almost 75.7 per cent of the total number interviewed, with 15.1 per cent of Malays, 6.6 per cent of Indians and the remaining (2.6 per cent) respondents from other ethnic groups. Respondents also had different educational levels, ranging from those with primary education or below (1.1 per cent) to those with tertiary education and higher (60.8 per cent). For the data analysis, we divided the 1,905 respondents into four income brackets, and there were sufficient numbers for each income bracket (in Singapore Dollars) as follows: 241 (low – below $3,000), 634 (medium low – $3,000 to $7,999), 725 (medium high – $8,000 to $14,999) and 305 (high – those earning $15,000 and more). The rationale will be discussed later in the data analyses section.

Representativeness of sample

Since the 2022 QOL Survey was for Singapore citizens only, the representativeness of the sample was examined by comparing important demographic characteristics of age, gender and race with those of the Singapore citizen population in 2021 (Department of Statistics Singapore, 2023a, b, c, d). There was a good balance of males and females in the sample, and the distribution was very close to that of the total population. The age distributions of the sample and Singapore's total population were quite dissimilar, with a slight overrepresentation of the below 50 years age groups: 5.9 per cent over representation of the "20 to 29 years" age group (16.1 per cent for the Singapore citizen population versus 22 per cent for our sample), 6.7 per cent over representation of the "30 to 39 years" age group (18.4 per cent for the Singapore citizen population versus 25.1 per cent for our sample) and 5.9 per cent overrepresentation of the "40 to 49 years" age group (18.5 per cent for the Singapore citizen population versus 24.4 per cent for our sample). There was a slight underrepresentation of Singaporeans aged 60 years and above: 7.6 per cent underrepresentation of the "60 to 69 years" age group (16.1 per cent for the Singapore citizen population versus 8.6 per cent for our sample), and 10.8 percent underrepresentation of the "70 years and above" age group (12.6 per cent for the Singapore citizen population versus 1.8 per cent for our sample). In terms of race, the distributions of the sample and the Singapore citizen population were fairly close. The Malays were very slightly overrepresented: 2.5 per cent overrepresentation for Malays (12.6 per cent for the Singapore citizen population versus 15.1 per cent for our sample). Indians had a very slight (1.8 per cent) underrepresentation (8.4 per cent for the Singapore citizen population versus 6.6 per cent for our sample).

In view of the slight over- and underrepresentations, we weighted the sample according to data on Singapore citizens in 2021 from the Department of Statistics (Department of Statistics Singapore, 2023a, b, c, d) to make the sample representative of the

Singapore citizen population. Key dimensions of the Singapore citizen population in terms of age, gender and race were used to weight the survey sample. The demographic profiles (for the weighted and unweighted datasets) are summarized in Table 1.3.

We also conducted a series of data analyses such as frequency distributions, cross-tabulations and computation of mean scores using the original and weighted samples to see whether there were any significant deviations in the responses due to the slight over- and underrepresentations. Our analyses revealed some differences in the results derived from both sets of samples. Given that there were slight discrepancies in the characteristics of our sample and the population of Singapore citizens, and there were some differences in responses between the original and the weighted

Table 1.3 Breakdown of sample respondents by gender, age and race for weighted and unweighted datasets

Demographics	Unweighted Dataset of Respondents		Weighted Dataset of Respondents	Singapore Citizens (SingStat 2021 statistics)
Breakdown of sample respondents by age				
Age	n	%	%	%
20–29	419	22.0	17.6	16.1
30–39	479	25.1	20.1	18.4
40–49	465	24.4	20.2	18.5
50–59	344	18.1	19.9	18.2
60–69	164	8.6	17.7	16.2
Above 70	34	1.8	4.6	12.6
Total	1905	100.0	100.0	100.0
Breakdown of sample respondents by gender				
Gender	n	%	%	%
Male	972	51.0	47.7	48.5
Female	933	49.0	52.3	51.5
Total	1905	100.0	100.0	100.0
Breakdown of sample respondents by race				
Race	n	%	%	%
Chinese	1442	75.7	74.2	76.0
Malay	288	15.1	14.7	12.6
Indian	126	6.6	7.6	8.4
Others	49	2.6	3.5	3.0
Total	1905	100%	100%	100.0%

datasets, the weighted sample would be used for data analyses to ensure generalizability of our results.

Data analyses

In the following chapters, descriptive analyses involving frequency tabulations, means comparisons, cross-tabulations and the construction of indices will be presented for the data collected. Where appropriate, we conducted correlation analyses to examine the relationships among the variables investigated, regression analyses to examine the impact of input variables on wellbeing outcomes and clustering analysis to differentiate the various types of Singaporeans. We also provided comparisons to our previous QOL surveys (2011 and 2016) in Singapore and other research studies where applicable.

We tested for individual differences among demographic groups using gender, marital status, age, education, and monthly household income. Race was not used for analysis due to the very small number of respondents in two out of the four racial groups in Singapore. This was also the case in our past QOL Surveys (2011 and 2016). For education, we have three levels, namely, low (those with no formal education or primary school education), medium (those with secondary/GCE O Level, postsecondary/ITE or GCE A Level/Diploma qualifications) and high (those with university or postgraduate degrees). For monthly household incomes (in Singapore Dollars) we have four income levels: low (those earning less than $3,000), medium low (those earning $3,000 to $7,999), medium high (those earning $8,000 to $14,999) and high (those earning $15,000 and more). These levels were decided based on statistics from the General Household Survey 2015 (Department of Statistics Singapore, 2015). The median household income from work was $8,666 (Department of Statistics Singapore, 2015) and the income ceiling to qualify for public housing (executive condominium) was $15,000. For marital status, we compared the responses of single and married people as the numbers for those who are divorced, widowed or separated were too small.

Overview of book chapters

In Chapter 2, we analyze the cognitive aspects of wellbeing by looking at Singaporeans' satisfaction with life, their satisfaction with various life domains and their evaluations of their lives currently and five years into the future. In Chapter 3, we focus on the affective aspects of wellbeing (e.g., happiness, enjoyment, achievement, control and purpose) and psychological flourishing. In Chapter 4, we explore the income-happiness equation by assessing the impact of household income on wellbeing outcomes such as happiness, enjoyment, achievement, control, purpose, satisfaction with life and satisfaction with the overall QOL. We also discuss the economic wellbeing of Singaporeans in terms of whether one has enough money to buy the things one need, to fulfill monthly loan commitments, to do things one wants to do and to make a major purchase.

In Chapter 5, we use the List of Values (LOV) to evaluate the importance of certain personal values to Singaporeans and tracked the changes over time. We also conduct regression analyses to examine the impact of the LOV on Singaporeans' wellbeing. In Chapter 6, we discuss the value orientations of Singaporeans such as family values, sustainability, traditionalism and materialism. We also employ clustering analysis to define groups of Singaporeans based on these value orientations. We then evaluate their wellbeing based on these clusters.

In Chapter 7, we examine Singaporeans' satisfaction with their democratic rights as citizens and their views on various aspects of politics. We then show how these attitudes may influence the wellbeing of Singaporeans. In Chapter 8, the multifaceted impact of the COVID-19 pandemic on the wellbeing of Singaporeans will be discussed. We focus on the economic impact, health risks, familial factors and social disruptions that Singaporeans had to deal with during the pandemic. In Chapter 9, we conclude with an overview of the key findings of the 2022 QOL Survey, and how the QOL Surveys in Singapore provide unique insights into the research on happiness and wellbeing. We also propose directives for future research in these areas.

References

Corrupt Practices Investigation Bureau. (2021). *Political and economic risk consultancy limited.* Corrupt Practices Investigation Bureau. Retrieved 29 June 2022, from www.cpib.gov.sg/research-room/international-rankings/political-and-economic-risk-consultancy-limited/

Department of Statistics (DOS) Singapore. (2015). (rep.). General household survey 2015 (pp. 1–469). Retrieved 30 April 2023, from www.singstat.gov.sg/-/media/files/publications/ghs/ghs2015/ghs2015.pdf.

Department of Statistics (DOS) Singapore. (2022a). *Population trends 2022.* Retrieved 24 April 2023, from www.singstat.gov.sg/publications/population/population-trends

Department of Statistics (DOS) Singapore. (2022b). *Education, language spoken and literacy–latest data.* Department of Statistics (DOS) Singapore. Retrieved 23 June 2022, from www.singstat.gov.sg/find-data/search-by-theme/population/education-language-spoken-and-literacy/latest-data

Department of Statistics (DOS) Singapore. (2022c). *Death and life expectancy–latest data.* Department of Statistics (DOS) Singapore. Retrieved 23 June 2022, from www.singstat.gov.sg/find-data/search-by-theme/population/death-and-life-expectancy/latest-data

Department of Statistics (DOS) Singapore. (2022d). *Singapore economy.* Retrieved 24 April 2023 from www.singstat.gov.sg/modules/infographics/economy

Department of Statistics (DOS) Singapore. (2022e). *Key household income trends, 2022.* Retrieved 22 April 2023, from www.singstat.gov.sg/-/media/files/publications/households/pp-s29.ashx

Freedom House. (2022a). *Global freedom status.* Retrieved 10 March 2023, from https://freedomhouse.org/explore-the-map?type=fiw&year=2022&status%5Bpartly-free%5D=partly-free&status%5Bfree%5D=free

Freedom House. (2022b). *Singapore: Freedom in the World 2022 Country Report.* Retrieved 10 March 2023, from https://freedomhouse.org/country/singapore/freedom-world/2022

GNH Centre Bhutan. (n.d.). *What is Gross National Happiness?* Retrieved 28 February 2023, from www.gnhcentrebhutan.org/

Helliwell, J. F., Layard, R., Sachs, J. D., Neve, J.-E. D., Aknin, L. B., & Wang, S. (2021, 20 March). *World Happiness Report 2021.* The World Happiness Report. Retrieved 6 July 2022, from https://worldhappiness.report/ed/2021/

The Heritage Foundation. (2022a). *Country rankings: World & global economy rankings on economic freedom.* 2023 Index of Economic Freedom. Retrieved 29 June 2022, from www.heritage.org/index/ranking

The Heritage Foundation. (2022b). *Singapore economy: Population, GDP, inflation, business, trade, FDI, corruption.* 2023 Index of Economic Freedom. Retrieved 29 June 2022, from www.heritage.org/index/country/singapore

Huang, C. (2023, 25 January). Core inflation flat at 5.1% in December, likely to remain elevated for some months. *Straits Times.* Retrieved 26 April 2023, from www.straitstimes.com/business/singapore-core-inflation-flat-at-51-in-december-2022-meets-official-forecast

Mathews, M., Suhaini, S., Hou, M., & Tan, A. (2021, April). *The COVID-19 pandemic in Singapore, one year on: Population attitudes and sentiments*. Institute of Policy Studies. Retrieved 17 October 2021 from https://lkyspp.nus.edu.sg/docs/default-source/ips/working-paper-40_the-covid-19-pandemic-in-singapore-one-year-on-population-attitudes-and-sentiments.pdf

Ministry of Manpower Singapore. (2023, 15 March). Statement on labour market developments in 2022. Retrieved 26 April 2023, from www.mom.gov.sg/newsroom/press-releases/2023/0315-labour-market-report-2022

O'Neill, A. (2022). *Singapore: Inflation rate from 1987 to 2027*. Statista. Retrieved 29 June 2022, from www.statista.com/statistics/379423/inflation-rate-in-singapore/

Social Progress Imperative. (2021). *2021 Social Progress Index executive summary*. Retrieved 30 June 2022, from www.socialprogress.org/static/9e62d6c031f30344f34683259839760d/2021%20Social%20Progress%20Index%20Executive%20Summary-compressed_0.pdf

Social Progress Imperative. (2022). *2022 Social Progress Index map Singapore*. Retrieved 30 June 2022, from www.socialprogress.org/?tab=2&code=SGP

Stiglitz, J. E., Sen, A., & Fitoussi, J.-P. (2009). *Report by the Commission on the Measurement of Economic Performance and Social Progress*. European Commission. Retrieved 28 February 2023, from https://ec.europa.eu/eurostat/documents/8131721/8131772/Stiglitz-Sen-Fitoussi-Commission-report.pdf

Transparency International. (2017). *2017 Corruption Perceptions Index*. Retrieved 6 July 2022, from www.transparency.org/en/cpi/2017

Transparency International. (2021). *2021 Corruption Perceptions Index*. Retrieved 29 June 2022, from www.transparency.org/en/cpi/2021

United Nations Development Programme. (2023). *Human Development Index (HDI) by country 2023*. World Population Review. Retrieved 28 February 2023, from https://worldpopulationreview.com/country-rankings/hdi-by-country

2   A holistic perspective of wellbeing I

Satisfaction with life and life domains

Research on happiness has been thriving for many years. While there are many diverse definitions of happiness, one prominent stream of research conceptualizes happiness as subjective well-being (SWB). This is a multifaceted concept that encompasses both cognitive and affective perceptions of one's life as a whole and also specific domains of life (Diener, 1984, 2006; Myers & Diener, 1995). Cognitive perceptions are related to one's life satisfaction, evaluation of life domains and how one thinks and feels about these aspects of life. Affective perceptions focus on the presence of positive emotions or the absence of negative emotions. Higher levels of life satisfaction and positive emotions are anticipated to lead to greater levels of subjective wellbeing. Subjective wellbeing is also enhanced when one finds fulfillment and purpose in what they are doing. This eudemonic approach considers the contributions of the intrinsic meaning of life and the fulfillment of life goals and skills (Seligman, 2012), engagement and other aspects of psychological flourishing (Diener & Biswas-Diener, 2008) and positive functioning (Sen, 1993).

In our QOL Surveys, we have incorporated a holistic perspective of wellbeing in our theoretical conceptualization, measurement and analysis. In this chapter, we discuss the cognitive aspects of wellbeing (e.g., satisfaction with life and satisfaction with specific life domains). The affective aspects (e.g., happiness and enjoyment) and psychological flourishing will be discussed in Chapter 3. Cognitive wellbeing (or life satisfaction) is derived from a conscious judgment and evaluation of one's quality of life. This is often an information-based evaluation, and may reflect

DOI: 10.4324/9781003399650-2

the gap between one's actual experience and the expectations of a better or ideal life. Various types of outcomes have been used in measuring life satisfaction (see Diener and Suh [1997] for a comprehensive review). These outcomes could be objective and quantitative statistics such as per capita income, mortality rates, years of formal schooling which are used in the Human Development Index. They could be more subjective and perceptual measures in assessing the QOL as experienced by individuals within a society. These could include noneconomic indicators such as relationships, feelings of belonging and long-term goals (Diener & Tov, 2012). For our study, the measures used to assess the cognitive aspects of wellbeing are the Satisfaction with Life Scale, the Cantril Ladder and satisfaction with life domains. In the chapters to follow, the life satisfaction scores for the Satisfaction with Life scale will be used as a key wellbeing outcome in our analyses.

The "Satisfaction with Life" scale

For the 2022 and 2016 QOL Surveys, we used the five-item "Satisfaction with Life" scale developed by Diener et al. (1985). This is an established scale that has been used in many research studies. We also tested its reliability for the Singaporean context. Previously, for the 2016 QOL Survey, a factor analysis on the scale items showed the items loading on one factor with 66.23 per cent of the variance and a Cronbach alpha of 0.860, which indicated a good level of reliability. For the 2022 QOL Survey, the factor analysis also extracted a single factor (with a Cronbach alpha of 0.91) which accounted for 72.99 per cent of the variance. Our analyses have thus confirmed its unidimensionality and good reliability. For the overall sample in 2022 (see Table 2.1), Singaporeans were generally satisfied with their lives (the highest mean of 4.18) and felt they had the important things in life (the second-highest mean of 4.04). Compared to the 2016 QOL Survey, the individual means and the composite mean score for 2022 have decreased.

The Cantril Ladder

The Cantril Self-Anchoring Scale (Cantril, 1965) has been used in several Gallup polls. The World Happiness Report 2023 also used this scale to measure the happiness of respondents in 137 countries.

Table 2.1 Frequency distribution of responses to the Satisfaction with Life scale (2016 and 2022)

Items		1 %	2 %	3 %	4 %	5 %	6 %	Mean
1. In most ways my life is close to my ideal	2016	0.9	6.0	9.4	35.2	45.2	3.3	4.28
	2022	5.7	10.0	19.4	31.6	25.0	8.3	3.85
2. The conditions of my life are excellent	2016	0.8	5.4	10.2	33.5	45.9	4.2	4.31
	2022	4.4	8.5	15.6	34.3	28.7	8.5	4.00
3. I am satisfied with my life	2016	0.7	4.0	7.4	25.9	55.5	6.5	4.51
	2022	4.2	6.7	13.4	29.9	34.3	11.5	4.18
4. So far I have gotten the important things I want in life	2016	0.9	6.0	8.3	27.3	50.1	7.4	4.42
	2022	4.9	7.7	16.3	30.4	30.9	9.8	4.04
5. If I could live my life over, I would change almost nothing	2016	3.5	13.7	18.6	21.2	37.5	5.5	3.92
	2022	9.1	15.4	23.8	22.2	21.2	8.3	3.56
Composite Mean Score	2016							4.29
	2022							3.92

Notes: 1=Strongly disagree, 2=Disagree 3=Slightly disagree, 4=Slightly agree, 5=Agree, 6=Strongly Agree.

Respondents were asked to evaluate their present and future (five years from now) lives on a ladder with numbers 0 (worst possible life) to 10 (best possible life), and their responses reflect a cognitive evaluation of their lives.

As seen in Figure 2.1, in 2011, Singaporeans perceived themselves to be approximately on the 4th rung of the ladder, and expected their lives to deteriorate to the lower 3rd rung in five years' time. However, contrary to their expectations, Singaporeans' ratings of their lives improved significantly in 2016 to just above the 6th rung, three steps above the forecasted scores. They were also relatively optimistic about the future, as they expected themselves to improve to nearly the 7th rung in five years' time. This prediction turned out to be unrealized as Singaporeans' score on the Cantril Ladder remained on the 6th rung in 2022. Comparing the mean scores between Singaporeans' evaluation of their lives in 2016 and 2022, however, revealed a significant decline in cognitive wellbeing. Yet, Singaporeans remained hopeful of their future as they expected their lives to improve to a mean rating of 6.45 by 2027.

Although Singaporeans had lower scores on the Cantril Ladder in the 2022 QOL Survey compared to 2016, Singapore continued to rank fairly well in the World Happiness Report 2023, which used

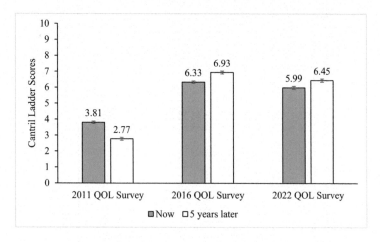

Figure 2.1 Comparison of Cantril Ladder scores across the 2011, 2016 and 2022 QOL Surveys.

Note: Error bar shows 95 per cent confidence intervals. Cantril Ladder scores ranged from 0 (worst possible life) to 10 (best possible life).

a three-year average (2020–2022) of the Cantril Ladder scores to rank 137 countries. Singapore was ranked 25th, with an average value of 6.587 (the average is based on 2020 and 2021 data only), against Finland, which was ranked as the happiest country with an average value of 7.804 (Helliwell et al., 2023).

Satisfaction with life domains and satisfaction with overall quality of life

In assessing life satisfaction, one approach would be to divide one's life into distinct domains such as family, work, studies, health and so on. This is known as "domain satisfaction", which encompasses one's evaluation of certain important aspects of life (Veenhoven, 2012). Satisfaction with each of these domains can be individually assessed and sometimes aggregated to provide a sense of one's overall wellbeing (Kau & Wang, 1995). These could include income, family relations, job and health (Easterlin, 2006). Studies have shown that satisfaction with life was positively associated with satisfaction within each of these four domains, with the highest weight given to family and social relations, followed by job, health and income (Kapteyn et al., 2010). Other researchers have found that one's wellbeing was enhanced by having strong interpersonal relationships, such as family life and marriage (Campbell, 1976), and friendships (Demir & Ozdemir, 2010). Having good physical and mental health also had a positive influence on people's happiness and life satisfaction (Borooah, 2006).

Respondents in the 2022 QOL Survey were asked to indicate their satisfaction with their life domains using a scale as follows: 1 for "very dissatisfied", 2 for "dissatisfied", 3 for "somewhat dissatisfied", 4 for "somewhat satisfied", 5 for "satisfied" and 6 for "very satisfied". A higher score indicated a greater degree of satisfaction. The 15 life domains were housing, friendships, marriage or romantic relationship, relationship with parents, relationship with children, relationship with brothers or sisters, relationship with neighbors, standard of living, household income, health, education attained, job (for those who are working full time), studies (for those who are studying), leisure activities or entertainment and spiritual life. Table 2.2 shows the distribution of responses for the 15 life domains and satisfaction with overall QOL. Singaporeans were most satisfied with the relationships with their children, parents and siblings, their marriage or romantic relationships

Table 2.2 Frequency distribution of responses to satisfaction with life domains and satisfaction with overall quality of life (2022)

Rank	Life Domains	1 %	2 %	3 %	4 %	5 %	6 %	Mean
1	Relationship with your children	1.9	2.4	6.0	19.1	39.2	31.4	4.86
2	Relationship with your parents	2.1	2.2	7.7	20.2	38.8	29.0	4.78
3	Relationship with brothers/sisters	3.0	3.0	8.5	24.8	36.0	24.7	4.62
4	Marriage/Romantic relationship	5.3	3.9	9.4	19.8	33.6	28.1	4.57
5	Spiritual life	1.6	3.1	9.5	30.3	35.1	20.4	4.55
6	Studies (if studying part/full time)	4.0	3.3	9.3	24.5	38.2	20.7	4.51
7	Leisure activities/entertainment	2.5	3.3	9.5	30.7	37.4	16.7	4.47
8	Friendships	2.6	2.6	8.8	33.7	39.4	12.9	4.43
9	Housing	4.3	3.8	9.1	30.0	40.8	11.9	4.35
10	Education attained	2.9	4.0	12.3	30.3	39.1	11.5	4.33
11	Job (if you are working)	4.6	5.5	10.3	28.8	35.3	15.6	4.31
12	Relationship with neighbors	3.0	3.9	9.4	37.9	36.7	9.1	4.29
13	Health	2.6	4.5	13.4	30.8	40.0	8.7	4.27
14	Standard of living	4.7	6.0	13.3	30.8	35.6	9.7	4.16
15	Household income	5.5	6.6	16.1	32.6	30.9	8.3	4.01
	Satisfaction with overall quality of life	3.1	4.8	8.8	31.3	38.9	13.1	4.38

Notes: 1=Very dissatisfied, 2=Dissatisfied, 3=Somewhat dissatisfied, 4=Somewhat satisfied, 5=Satisfied, 6=Very satisfied.

and their spiritual lives. They were most dissatisfied with their household incomes, standard of living, health, relationships with neighbors and jobs (if they were working).

Table 2.3 shows the mean ratings of satisfaction with life domains for the years 2011, 2016 and 2022. Out of the 15 life domains, the top eight most satisfied domains were highly consistent across the three surveys over a period of 11 years. In all three surveys, Singaporeans were most satisfied with their relationship

Table 2.3 Mean ratings of satisfaction with life domains and satisfaction with overall quality of life (2011, 2016 and 2022)

Life Domains	2022 Mean	2016 Mean	2011 Mean
Relationship with your children	4.86 (1)	5.14 (1)	5.32 (1)
Relationship with your parents	4.78 (2)	5.02 (2)	5.17 (2)
Relationship with brothers/sisters	4.62 (3)	4.93 (3)	5.09 (3)
Marriage/Romantic relationship	4.57 (4)	4.72 (6)	4.88 (4)
Spiritual life	4.55 (5)	4.80 (4)	4.74 (7)
Studies (if studying part/full time)	4.51 (6)	4.44 (14)	4.75 (6)
Leisure activities/ entertainment	4.47 (7)	4.70 (8)	4.74 (7)
Friendships	4.43 (8)	4.74 (5)	4.84 (5)
Housing	4.35 (9)	4.72 (6)	4.69 (10)
Education attained	4.33 (10)	4.45 (13)	4.45 (14)
Job (if you are working)	4.31 (11)	4.54 (12)	4.65 (11)
Relationship with neighbors	4.29 (12)	4.64 (9)	4.61 (12)
Health	4.27 (13)	4.62 (10)	4.72 (9)
Standard of living	4.16 (14)	4.55 (11)	4.50 (13)
Household income	4.01 (15)	4.19 (15)	4.34 (15)
Satisfaction with overall quality of life	4.38	4.81	4.83

Notes: Each domain was measured on a 6-point scale: 1 = Very Dissatisfied, 2 = Dissatisfied, 3 = Somewhat Dissatisfied, 4 = Somewhat satisfied, 5 = Satisfied, 6 = Very Satisfied. Numbers in parentheses indicate ranking based on highest to lowest mean ratings.

with their children, followed by their relationship with their parents and then their siblings. Satisfaction with one's marriage or romantic relationship ranked 4th for both 2011 and 2022, while it slipped to the 6th berth in 2016. The 4th spot in 2016 was taken by satisfaction with one's spiritual life, which occupied the 7th spot in 2011 and the 5th spot in 2022. Satisfaction with friends occupied the 5th position in both the 2011 and 2016 surveys, while this domain dropped to the 8th position in 2022. Satisfaction with one's studies ranked 6th in 2022. While it was also ranked 6th in 2011, this domain dropped drastically to the 14th position in 2016. Singaporeans' satisfaction with the leisure activities and entertainment domain hovered around the same spots, ranking 7th in 2022, joint 7th (with spiritual life) in 2011 and 8th in 2016.

Satisfaction with the housing domain fell to the 9th position in 2022 from its joint 6th position (with marriage or romantic relationship) in 2016; this domain ranked 10th in 2011. At 10th place in 2022 was the domain of education attained, which increased from the 14th spot in 2011 to the 13th spot in 2016. Satisfaction with one's job, however, was ranked similarly across the years, ranking 11th in 2022 and 2011 and 12th in 2016. After climbing three positions from 12th in 2011 to 9th in 2016, one's satisfaction with neighbors declined to the 12th spot once again in 2022. The domain of satisfaction with health faced a steady decline over the years, from 9th in 2011 to 10th in 2016 and to 13th in 2022. Similarly, satisfaction with one's standard of living has not been highly ranked over the last 11 years. It ranked 13th in 2011, increased to 11th in 2016, and got worse in 2022 by dropping to the 14th position. Finally, the domain of household income consistently ranked last (15th) across all three surveys.

Generally, from 2011 to 2022, Singaporeans were less satisfied with all life domains and their overall quality of life. Apart from satisfaction with studies, the decreases in mean ratings were all statistically significant. While this paints a gloomy picture of Singaporeans' satisfaction with specific life domains, there is a silver lining. All the mean scores in 2022 were above 4 and in the "satisfied" spectrum.

Sources of individual differences on satisfaction with life, Cantril Ladder and satisfaction with life domains

In research studies on life satisfaction, they usually analyze how demographic variables are correlated with certain wellbeing outcomes. For example, age, education, income, race, employment and marital status have been found to be correlated at varying degrees to life satisfaction (e.g., Blanchflower & Oswald, 2000; Oswald, 1997). However, these correlations tended to be weak, with less than 10 per cent of the variance explained (Andrews & Withey, 1974; Davis et al., 1982; Michalos, 1985; Veenhoven, 1984). The results of the impact of demographic variables are often mixed and dependent on the social and cultural contexts in which the studies are carried out. Nonetheless, for the QOL Surveys in Singapore, we usually present and discuss the sources of individual differences due to demographics as they may provide some additional insights into what matters for various segments of Singaporeans.

As the Satisfaction with Life Scale had good internal consistency, we aggregated the responses on the five items by taking their means (see Table 2.4). Males and married respondents had higher scores for satisfaction with life. Positive associations between satisfaction with life with education and household income were also found. Those who were more highly educated and had higher household incomes were more satisfied. Age was negatively associated with Satisfaction with Life scale scores, whereby older respondents were less satisfied with life than the younger ones.

For the scores on the Cantril Ladder, we found strong individual differences across the different demographics. Males rated their lives to be significantly better than females did, although both genders expected similar scores on the ladder in five years' time. As compared to the singles, married respondents perceived their lives to be better now and in five years' time. On age, the main source of differences in respondents' evaluation of their lives now stemmed from Singaporeans in the age group of 20 to 29 years, who perceived they had the worst possible life compared to the other age groups. Singaporeans' perception of their lives five years later painted a wholly different story. We found a negative association between age and respondents' expected score on the ladder five years from now. Older Singaporeans were more likely to report lower ladder scores five years from now. Finally, those who were more educated and had higher household incomes rated their lives to be better now, as well as in the future.

Table 2.5 shows the sources of individual differences for the top three most satisfied life domains for Singaporeans in

Table 2.4 Sources of individual differences for Satisfaction with Life Scale and Cantril Ladder (2022)

Demographics	Satisfaction with Life	Ladder (Now)	Ladder (5 years later)
Gender			
- Male	3.98	6.12	6.46
- Female	3.87	5.87	6.44
- *F*-Stats	**4.41**	**5.95**	0.04
- *p*	**.036**	**.015**	.851
Marital Status			
- Single	3.68	5.47	6.18
- Married	4.08	6.31	6.61
- *F*-Stats	**58.51**	**65.78**	**16.70**
- *p*	**< .001**	**< .001**	**< .001**
Age			
- 20–29	3.99	5.63	6.53
- 30–39	4.13	6.16	6.85
- 40–49	3.86	6.05	6.51
- 50–59	3.87	6.04	6.41
- 60–69	3.78	6.00	5.99
- 70–79	3.82	6.03	5.91
- *F*-Stats	**4.46**	**2.33**	**6.41**
- *p*	**< .001**	.040	**< .001**
Education			
- Low	3.69	5.44	5.79
- Medium	3.85	5.71	6.26
- High	4.04	6.30	6.75
- *F*-Stats	**14.20**	**26.29**	**27.87**
- *p*	**< .001**	**< .001**	**< .001**
Household Income			
- Low	3.47	5.01	5.56
- Low-Medium	3.77	5.59	6.10
- Medium-High	4.08	6.36	6.80
- High	4.30	6.87	7.19
- *F*-Stats	**35.53**	**50.27**	**36.92**
- *p*	**< .001**	**< .001**	**< .001**

Note: Bold figures indicate significance.

Table 2.5 Sources of individual differences for top three most satisfied life
domains (2022)

Demographics	1st domain Relationship with children	2nd domain Relationship with parents	3rd domain Relationship with brothers/ sisters
Gender			
- Male	4.99	4.82	4.68
- Female	4.93	4.76	4.56
- *F*-Stats	0.91	1.18	3.85
- *p*	.340	.277	.050
Marital status			
- Single	4.73	4.55	4.40
- Married	4.97	4.93	4.75
- *F*-Stats	1.80	**42.81**	**35.32**
- *p*	.180	**< .001**	**< .001**
Age			
- 20–29	4.81	4.66	4.62
- 30–39	5.13	4.87	4.70
- 40–49	4.97	4.72	4.56
- 50–59	4.91	4.89	4.57
- 60–69	4.80	4.74	4.61
- 70–79	5.32	5.00	4.79
- *F*-Stats	**3.89**	**2.30**	0.88
- *p*	**.002**	**.043**	.493
Education			
- Low	4.79	4.69	4.46
- Medium	4.98	4.73	4.57
- High	5.03	4.84	4.70
- *F*-Stats	**4.52**	2.59	**5.68**
- *p*	**.011**	.075	**.003**
Household Income			
- Low	4.72	4.58	4.39
- Low-Medium	4.79	4.70	4.52
- Medium-High	4.97	4.83	4.66
- High	5.29	5.04	4.96
- *F*-Stats	**10.86**	**7.80**	11.85
- *p*	**< .001**	**< .001**	**< .001**

Note: Bold figures indicate significance.

2022: relationships with (1) children; (2) parents and (3) siblings. Females and males did not differ in their satisfaction across the three domains. For marital status, the weighted dataset included 40 respondents who self-identified as "single" and having children. Married respondents were significantly more satisfied with their relationships with their parents and siblings. While satisfaction with siblings did not differ across different ages, age had a significant effect on how satisfied Singaporeans were with the relationship with their children and parents. There was a significant upward trend in the domain of relationship with children, as Singaporeans tended to be more satisfied with this domain as they got older. Similarly, the main source of age differences in the domain of relationship with parents came from respondents in their 20s, who were less satisfied with the relationships with their parents than some older age groups (i.e., those in their 30s or 50s). Levels of satisfaction with the relationships with one's children, parents and siblings were strongly associated with the respondents' highest level of education attained. Those who were highly educated were more satisfied with the relationships with their children, parents and siblings. Finally, there was also a positive trend between respondents' household income and their satisfaction with these three life domains.

Table 2.6 shows the sources of individual differences for the top three most dissatisfied life domains for 2022. Females were less satisfied than males regarding household incomes and health, while the two genders did not differ on satisfaction with standard of living. As compared to those who are married, singles were significantly less satisfied across all three domains. The age effect was varied. Data analyses revealed a U-shaped association between age and satisfaction with household income and standard of living. Younger respondents (i.e., those in their 20s and 30s) were relatively satisfied with their household income and standard of living, but the satisfaction levels dipped among middle-aged respondents (i.e., 40s to 60s), and then rebounded among the elderly (i.e. those in their 70s). While there was also a significant age effect on satisfaction with health, most age groups actually reported similar levels of satisfaction except for one: those in their 60s who were the least satisfied with their health. Respondents who were less educated (or had lower household income) tended to be less satisfied with their household incomes, standard of living and health.

Table 2.6 Sources of individual differences for top three most dissatisfied life domains (2022)

Demographics	1st domain Household Income	2nd domain Standard of Living	3rd domain Health
Gender			
- Male	4.10	4.20	4.33
- Female	3.93	4.11	4.22
- *F*-Stats	**8.52**	2.49	**4.21**
- *p*	**0.004**	0.115	**0.040**
Marital status			
- Single	3.78	3.97	4.12
- Married	4.16	4.27	4.36
- *F*-Stats	**38.94**	**26.15**	**20.88**
- *p*	**< 0.001**	**< 0.001**	**< 0.001**
Age			
- 20–29	4.07	4.24	4.33
- 30–39	4.18	4.21	4.38
- 40–49	3.94	4.12	4.28
- 50–59	3.95	4.19	4.27
- 60–69	3.87	3.97	4.06
- 70–79	4.29	4.35	4.35
- *F*-Stats	**3.37**	**2.50**	**3.33**
- *p*	**0.005**	**0.029**	**0.005**
Education			
- Low	3.66	3.79	4.08
- Medium	3.84	4.03	4.14
- High	4.21	4.34	4.39
- *F*-Stats	**32.02**	**30.88**	**15.21**
- *p*	**< 0.001**	**< 0.001**	**< 0.001**
Household Income			
- Low	3.36	3.65	4.02
- Low-Medium	3.74	3.91	4.14
- Medium-High	4.22	4.35	4.38
- High	4.74	4.69	4.53
- *F*-Stats	**78.78**	**48.84**	**15.22**
- *p*	**< 0.001**	**< 0.001**	**< 0.001**

Bold figures indicate significance.

Conclusion

In the QOL Surveys through the years (2011, 2016 and 2022), economic (e.g., household income) and noneconomic (e.g., relationships) measures of life satisfaction have been used. Together, these measures provided a more well-rounded perspective on the key drivers of wellbeing. The 2022 QOL Survey score for Satisfaction with Life (a 5-point scale) was lower compared to 2016. Singaporeans' score on the Cantril Ladder remained on the 6th rung in 2022, and a comparison of the scores between 2016 and 2022 revealed a significant decline in this aspect of cognitive wellbeing. However, based on the average three-year (2020–2022) Cantril Ladder ratings of 137 countries worldwide, Singapore was ranked the 25th happiest country in the world (Helliwell et al., 2023). The scores for satisfaction with the 15 life domains have also dipped over the years since 2011. In terms of satisfaction with life domains, across the three surveys conducted in 2011 and 2016 and 2022, Singaporeans were most satisfied with their familial relationships, although satisfaction with "marriage/romantic relationships" was lower in 2016. Consistently, Singaporeans were most dissatisfied with their household income in three surveys across 11 years. Satisfaction with education improved greatly, climbing from one of the last few spots in 2011 (14th) and 2016 (13th) to 10th in 2022. Comparatively, Singaporeans' satisfaction with their standard of living and health took a hit in 2022, taking the last 2nd- and 3rd-to-last position, respectively, in 2022.

The influence of certain demographic variables on life satisfaction and satisfaction with particular life domains was investigated in the 2022 QOL Survey. Demographic differences for the Satisfaction with Life composite score mirrored those for the Satisfaction with Life Domains, except for the effect of age. Marital status, education and household income were the main driving forces accounting for the differences in satisfaction for the three top and bottom life domains that Singaporeans were satisfied with. Gender and age were also influential among the bottom three domains although less so among the top three domains.

References

Andrews, F.M., & Withey, S.B. (1974). "Developing measures of perceived life quality: Results from several national surveys". *Social Indicators Research*, *1*, 1–26.

Blanchflower, D.G., & Oswald, A.J. (2000). *Wellbeing over time in Britain and the USA*. Cambridge, MA: National Bureau of Economic Research.

Borooah, V.K. (2006). "What makes people happy? Some evidence from Northern Ireland". *Journal of Happiness Studies, 7*, 427–465.

Campbell, A. (1976). "Subjective measures of wellbeing". *American Psychologist, 31*, 117–124.

Cantril, H. (1965). *The pattern of human concerns*. New Brunswick, NJ: Rutgers University Press.

Davis, E.E., Fine-Davis, M., & Meehan, G. (1982). "Demographic determinants of perceived wellbeing in eight European countries". *Social Indicators Research, 10*, 341–335.

Demir, M., & Ozdemir, M. (2010). "Friendship, need satisfaction and happiness". *Journal of Happiness Studies, 11*, 243–259.

Diener, E. (1984). "Subjective wellbeing". *Psychological Bulletin, 95*(3), 542–575.

Diener, E., Emmons, R. A., Larsen, R. J., & Griffin, S. (1985). "The Satisfaction with Life Scale". *Journal of Personality Assessment, 49*, 71–75.

Diener, E. and Suh, M. (1997). "Subjective wellbeing and age: An international analysis". *Annual Review of Gerontology and Geriatrics, 17*, 304–324.

Diener, E. (2006). "Guidelines for national indicators of subjective wellbeing and ill-being". *Journal of Happiness Studies, 7*(4), 397–404

Diener, E., & Biswas-Diener, R. (2008). *Happiness: Unlocking the mysteries of psychological wealth.* New York: Blackwell Publishing.

Diener, E., & Tov, W. (2012). "National accounts of wellbeing". *Handbook of social indicators and quality of life research.* New York: Springer.

Easterlin, R.A. (2006). "Life cycle happiness and its sources: Intersections of psychology, economics, and demography". *Journal of Economic Psychology, 27*(4), 463–482

Helliwell, J., Layard, R., Sachs, J. D., De Neve, J.-E., Aknin, L., & Wang, S. (2023). *World happiness report 2023*. Sustainable Development Solutions Network. Retrieved from https://worldhappiness.report/.

Kapteyn, A., Smith, J.P., & van Soest, A. (2010). "Life satisfaction". In E. Diener, D. Kahneman, & J. Helliwell (eds.), *International differences in well-being* (pp. 70–104). Oxford, UK: Oxford University Press.

Kau, A.K., & Wang, S.H. (1995). "Assessing quality of life in Singapore: An exploratory study". *Social Indicators Research, 35*, 71–91.

Michalos, A.C. (1985). "Multiple discrepancies theory (MDT)". *Social Indicators Research, 16*, 347–414.

Myers, D.G., & Diener, E. (1995). "Who is happy?" *Psychological Science, 6*, 10–19.

Oswald, A.J. (1997). "Happiness and economic performance". *Economic Journal, 107*(445), 1815–1831.

Seligman, M. (2012). *Flourish: A visionary new understanding of happiness and wellbeing*. New York: Free Press.

Sen, A. (1993). "Capability and wellbeing". In M. Nussenbaum and A. Sen (eds.), *The quality of life* (pp. 30–53) Oxford, UK: Clarendon Press.

Veenhoven, R. (1984). *Conditions of happiness*. Holland: D. Reidel.

Veenhoven, R. (2012). "Happiness also known as 'life satisfaction' and 'subjective well-being'". *Handbook of social indicators and quality of life research*. New York: Springer.

3 A holistic perspective of wellbeing II

Affective aspects and psychological flourishing

In this chapter, we discuss the affective aspects of wellbeing such as happiness, enjoyment, achievement, control over important aspects of life, a sense of purpose in life and psychological flourishing. Individual differences in these wellbeing outcomes are also examined. When possible, comparisons are made with previous surveys in 2011 and 2016. Together with Chapter 2, these additional outcomes present a multifaceted perspective of the wellbeing of Singaporeans.

Happiness, enjoyment, achievement, control and purpose

Affective measures complement the cognitive measures by highlighting the positive emotions that contribute to a person's wellbeing such as happiness and enjoyment (Veenhoven, 2012). Meaning and purpose are also important contributors to the perceived significance and worth of one's life (Ryan & Deci, 2001; Seligman, 2012). Questions on happiness, enjoyment, and achievement are from the 2006 AsiaBarometer Survey (Inoguchi, 2006), and questions on control and purpose are from Tinkler and Hicks's (2011) scales for locus of control and sense of purpose. The 12-item Psychological Flourishing scale developed by Diener and Biswas-Diener (2008) was used in the 2016 QOL Survey. We used a shortened eight-item version for the 2022 QOL Survey. The scale has been used to classify respondents at different levels of psychological flourishing, from "extremely high flourishing" to "extremely low flourishing".

DOI: 10.4324/9781003399650-3

For an indication of how happy Singaporeans are, respondents were asked in the 2022 QOL Survey to respond to the question of "All things considered, would you say that you are happy these days?" using a rating scale of "1 = Very unhappy", "2 = Not too happy", "3 = Neither happy nor unhappy", "4 = Quite happy" and "5 = Very happy". We computed a Happiness Index through a two-step process. First, we obtained the sum of percentages of respondents who responded that they were happy (i.e. 4 or 5 on the scale). Second, we subtracted the proportion of respondents who were unhappy (i.e. 1 or 2 on the scale) from the percentage of happy respondents. To assess enjoyment, respondents were asked to respond to the question of "How often do you feel you are really enjoying life these days?" using a rating scale of "1 = Never", "2 = Rarely", "3 = Sometimes" and "4 = Often". Following the same two-step process, an Enjoyment Index was computed by subtracting the percentage of respondents who indicated that they never or rarely enjoy life (i.e., 1 or 2 on the scale) from the proportion who reported that they sometimes or often enjoy life (i.e., 3 or 4 on the scale). For achievement, respondents were asked to respond to the question of "How much do you feel you are accomplishing what you want out of your life?" using a rating scale of "1 = None", "2 = Very little", "3 = Some" and "4 = A great deal". To assess control, respondents were asked to respond to the question of "How much control do you feel you have over important aspects of your life?" using a scale of "1 = None", "2 = Very little", "3 = Some" and "4 = A great deal". For purpose, respondents were asked to respond to the question of "How much control do you feel you have a sense of purpose in your life?" using a scale of "1 = None", "2 = Very little", "3 = Some" and "4 = A great deal". Similar to the Enjoyment Index, an Achievement Index, a Purpose Index and a Control Index were computed by subtracting the proportion of those who responded "1" and "2" for each respective question from the proportion of those who responded "3" and "4". To give us a sense of how Singaporeans fared in these outcomes over time, we also compared our findings with the results from the 2011 QOL Survey (Tambyah & Tan, 2013) and 2016 QOL Survey (Tambyah & Tan, 2018).

As seen in Figure 3.1a, all three Indices were positive in value, indicating that more Singaporeans were happy, enjoying life, and achieving things in life than those who were not. However, we observed a worrying trend of decreasing happiness, enjoyment and achievement among Singaporeans from 2011 to 2022. Across

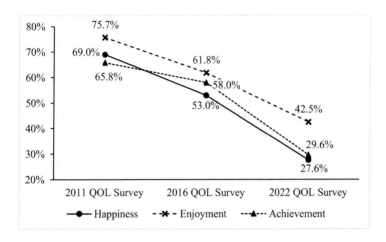

Figure 3.1a Indices of happiness, enjoyment and achievement (2011, 2016 and 2022).

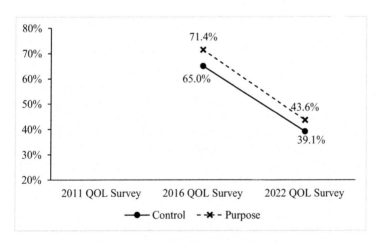

Figure 3.1b Indices of control and purpose (2016 and 2022).

11 years, the Happiness Index had the sharpest decline of about 41.4 per cent, falling from 69 per cent in 2011 to 27.6 per cent in 2022. The Enjoyment Index also fell steadily from 75.7 per cent in 2011 to 42.5 per cent in 2022. The Achievement Index dipped

slightly from 65.8 per cent in 2011 to 58.0 per cent in 2016 and almost halved in 2022 (29.6 per cent).

The Control and Purpose Indices were newly added in 2016, so we do not have data from 2011. From 2016 to 2022, we observed a 25.9 per cent decrease in the Control Index from 65 per cent to 39.1 per cent. The Purpose Index also faced a similar drop of 27.8 per cent from 2016 (71.4 per cent) to 2022 (43.6 per cent).

Overall, over the last 11 years, Singaporeans' wellbeing has been steadily decreasing from 2011 to 2016, and then to 2022. All five Indices were worse off in 2022 as compared to six years ago and 11 years ago. Notably, each of the five indices were strongly and positively correlated with each other ($r > 0.606$), suggesting that the affective aspects of wellbeing tended to spill over to one another. In other words, Singaporeans may work on improving one aspect of their wellbeing, and this could possibly elevate other aspects of their wellbeing.

Sources of individual differences for affective wellbeing outcomes

How do certain demographic variables correlate with measures of happiness, enjoyment, achievement, control and purpose? Researchers have examined sources of individual differences due to age (e.g., Blanchflower & Oswald, 2000; Oswald, 1997), social class (e.g., Inoguchi & Fujii, 2009), and marital status (e.g., Diener et al., 2000; Veroff et al., 1981). Results are often mixed depending on the social and cultural contexts of these studies.

To analyze the demographic differences in the 2022 QOL Survey, we compared the means of the different demographic subgroups. As the item on happiness was on a five-point scale (1 = Very unhappy, 5 = Very happy), while the questions on enjoyment, achievement, control and purpose were on a four-point scale, we first recoded the happiness question into a four-point scale by combining the responses of those who selected options 1 (very unhappy) and 2 (not too happy) into a single category.

Our 2022 QOL Survey showed that demographics (i.e., gender, marital status, age, education and household income) have a strong effect on affective wellbeing. All demographic differences were statistically significant, except for gender differences in enjoyment which was only marginally significant ($p = 0.059$). Males scored significantly higher on all five outcomes than females (Figure 3.2).

Marital status also had a significant effect, with married respondents reporting greater happiness, enjoyment, achievement, control and sense of purpose than the singles (Figure 3.3).

Aging had a positive effect on all five outcomes: happiness, enjoyment, achievement, control and sense of purpose. As Singaporeans got older, they tended to be happier, enjoyed life

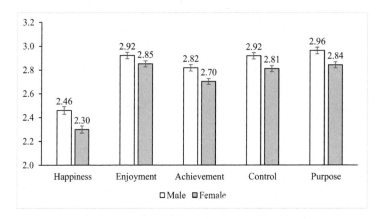

Figure 3.2 Gender differences for happiness, enjoyment, achievement, control and purpose (2022).

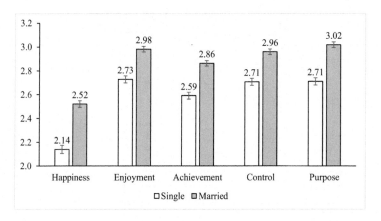

Figure 3.3 Marital status differences for happiness, enjoyment, achievement, control and purpose (2022).

more, felt they had achieved more, had more control and had a stronger sense of purpose (Figure 3.4). Education was positively correlated with all five outcomes (Figure 3.5). This holds true for household income as well (Figure 3.6).

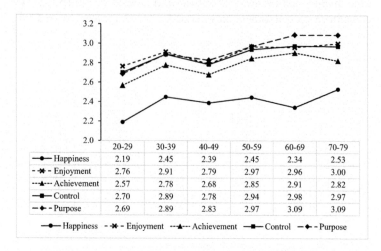

	20-29	30-39	40-49	50-59	60-69	70-79
Happiness	2.19	2.45	2.39	2.45	2.34	2.53
Enjoyment	2.76	2.91	2.79	2.97	2.96	3.00
Achievement	2.57	2.78	2.68	2.85	2.91	2.82
Control	2.70	2.89	2.78	2.94	2.98	2.97
Purpose	2.69	2.89	2.83	2.97	3.09	3.09

Figure 3.4 Age trend for happiness, enjoyment, achievement, control and purpose (2022).

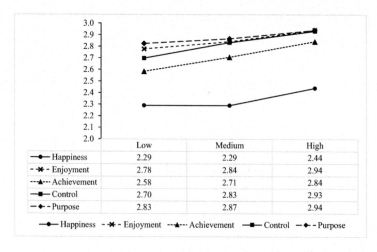

	Low	Medium	High
Happiness	2.29	2.29	2.44
Enjoyment	2.78	2.84	2.94
Achievement	2.58	2.71	2.84
Control	2.70	2.83	2.93
Purpose	2.83	2.87	2.94

Figure 3.5 Education trend for happiness, enjoyment, achievement, control and purpose (2022).

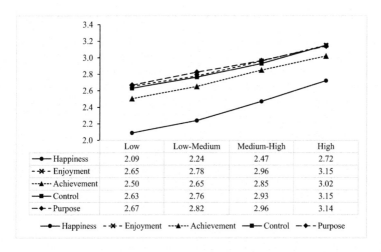

	Low	Low-Medium	Medium-High	High
Happiness	2.09	2.24	2.47	2.72
Enjoyment	2.65	2.78	2.96	3.15
Achievement	2.50	2.65	2.85	3.02
Control	2.63	2.76	2.93	3.15
Purpose	2.67	2.82	2.96	3.14

Figure 3.6 Household income trend for happiness, enjoyment, achievement, control and purpose (2022).

Thus, it appears that in Singapore, if one feels they have been happier, have enjoyed life more, have achieved more, have more control over important aspects of their lives and have more purpose in life, they are likely to be male, married, older, have more education and have a higher income.

Psychological flourishing

Psychological flourishing is an important aspect of wellbeing that has been well-documented (Hone et al., 2014). Psychological flourishing "goes beyond an individual's pursuit of her own happiness to include her contributions to society and the happiness of others" (Diener & Biswas-Diener, 2008, p. 241). The original 12-item Psychological Flourishing Scale measured aspects of psychological wealth and whether one's life had purpose and meaning (Diener and Biswas-Diener, 2008). Diener et al. (2010) revised this to an eight-item scale and renamed it the Flourishing Scale. This scale has been validated in various countries and contexts, for instance, in Egypt (Salama-Younes, 2017), France (Villieux et al., 2016), Japan (Sumi, 2014), New Zealand (Hone et al., 2014) and Portugal (Silva & Caetano, 2013). We compared the eight-item

Flourishing Scale scores across the three QOL Surveys conducted in 2011, 2016 and 2022. In all three QOL Surveys, we used a six-point scale (1 = Strongly Disagree, 6 = Strongly Agree) for consistency with other parts of the surveys. Participants' responses to each item were summed up to obtain a psychological flourishing score, which could range from 8 to 48. The distributions of the respective composite scores on psychological flourishing for 2011, 2016 and 2022 are shown in Figure 3.7.

Singaporeans' levels of psychological flourishing were significantly worse in 2022 than in 2011 and in 2016. While there was an improvement in psychological flourishing from 2011 ($M = 36.2$, $SD = 4.63$) to 2016 ($M = 37.07$, $SD = 4.57$), Singaporeans' psychological flourishing in 2022 ($M = 34.27$, $SD = 6.93$) reversed the gains in 2016 and even declined to below the level indicated in 2011.

Looking at the distributions of scores in Figure 3.7, we may gain some insights to which segments of Singaporeans fell behind in their psychological flourishing in 2022. In general, it appears that Singaporeans with relatively poorer psychological flourishing contributed the largest to the decline in 2022. The psychological flourishing scores in 2011, 2016 and 2022 were relatively

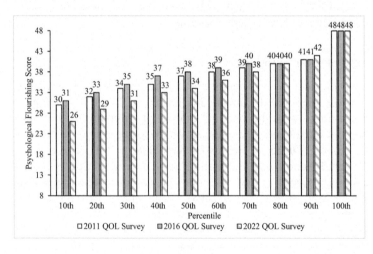

Figure 3.7 Distribution of Flourishing Scale scores by percentile for 2011, 2016 and 2022 QOL Surveys.

comparable from the 70th percentile and above. In other words, for the Singaporean population, those who had good psychological flourishing tended to have scores at similar levels across the three QOL Surveys. The divide began to widen in the middle and bottom echelons of the distributions. At the 60th percentile, Singaporeans in 2022 scored two to three points lower than in 2011 and 2016; from the 20th to 60th percentile, this discrepancy increased to three to four points. At the 10th percentile, Singaporeans in 2022 scored four points lower than in 2011 and five points lower than in 2016 – that is, if we compare Singaporeans with the lowest psychological flourishing scores across the three surveys, respondents in the 2022 QOL Survey were worse off than respondents in the 2011 and 2016 surveys.

Sources of individual differences for psychological flourishing

There were several significant individual differences in Singaporeans' psychological flourishing (see Figures 3.8 and 3.9). While no gender differences were found in the 2022 QOL Survey, married respondents tended to have better psychological flourishing than those who were single. We also found a positive linear education effect on psychological flourishing, with more educated respondents having greater psychological flourishing.

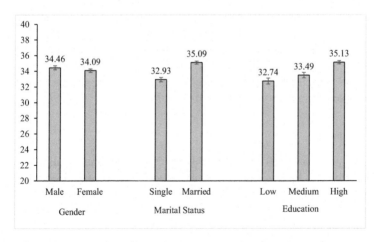

Figure 3.8 Individual differences across gender, marital status and education for Psychological Flourishing (2022).

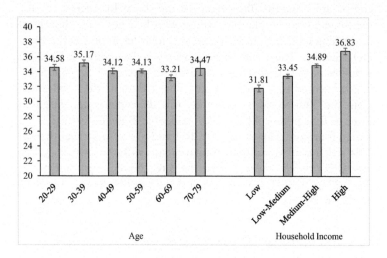

Figure 3.9 Individual differences across age and household income for Psychological Flourishing (2022).

As seen in Figure 3.9, there was also a significant positive association between household income and psychological flourishing. Respondents with higher household income tended to have better psychological flourishing. Although psychological flourishing also significantly differed across the different age groups, there was not a distinct age trend. Those between the ages of 60 and 69 years had the lowest psychological flourishing scores, while respondents in the 30 to 39 years age group had the highest psychological flourishing scores. Psychological flourishing of the other age groups fell in between the scores of those aged 30 to 39 years and 60 to 69 years.

Conclusion

Over the past 10 years (2011 to 2022), Singaporeans have become less happy, enjoyed life less and felt a decreased sense of achievement. Compared to the 2016 QOL Survey, Singaporeans also felt a sense of reduced control over their lives and lack of purpose in life.

Demographic had strong influences on Singaporeans' self-assessment of their happiness, enjoyment, achievement, control and purpose. Those who are male, married, older, have higher education and have higher income tend to have greater levels of happiness, enjoyment, achievement, control and purpose in their lives. While gender did not matter for the Enjoyment Index, as compared to females, males were happier, achieved more, had greater control and had a stronger sense of purpose in their lives.

Singaporeans seemed to have declined in psychological flourishing over the past 10 years from 2011 to 2022. Demographically, education, gender, household income and marital status contributed to differences in Singaporeans' assessment of their state of psychological flourishing.

References

Blanchflower, D.G., & Oswald, A.J. (2000). *Well-being over time in Britain and the USA*. Cambridge, MA: National Bureau of Economic Research.

Diener, E., Gohm, C.L., Suh, E.M., & Oishi, S. (2000). "Similarity of the relations between marital status and subjective well-being across cultures". *Journal of Cross-Cultural Psychology, 31*(4), 419–436.

Diener, E., & Biswas-Diener, R. (2008). *Happiness: Unlocking the mysteries of psychological wealth*. New York: Blackwell Publishing.

Diener. E., Wirtz, D., Tov, W., Prieto, C.K., Choi, D., Oishi, S., & Biswas-Diener, R. (2010). "New well-being measures: Short scales to assess flourishing and positive and negative feelings". *Social Indicators Research, 97*(2), 143–156.

Hone, L., Jarden, A., & Schofield, G. (2014). "Psychometric properties of the flourishing scale in New Zealand". *Social Indicators Research, 119*(2), 1031–1045.

Inoguchi, T. (2006). "AsiaBarometer, 2006". Retrieved from https://doi.org/10.3886/E163441V1

Inoguchi, T., & Fujii, S. (2009). "The quality of life in Japan". *Social Indicators Research, 92,* 227–262.

Oswald, A.J. (1997). "Happiness and economic performance". *Economic Journal, 107*(445), 1815–1831.

Ryan, R. M., & Deci, E. L. (2001). "To be happy or to be self-fulfilled: A review of research on hedonic and eudaemonic wellbeing". In S. Fiske (ed.), *Annual Review of Psychology* (vol. 52, pp. 141–166). Palo Alto, CA: Annual Reviews, Inc.

Salama-Younes, M. (2017). "Psychometric properties of the psychological flourishing scale in an Egyptian setting". *Journal of Psychology in Africa, 27*(4), 310–315.

Seligman, M. (2012). *Flourish: A visionary new understanding of happiness and wellbeing*. Hillsboro, OR: Altraria Book.

Silva, A.J., & Caetano, A. (2013). "Validation of the flourishing scale and scale of positive and negative experience in Portugal". *Social Indicators Research, 110*(2), 469–478.

Sumi, K. (2014). "Reliability and validity of Japanese versions of the flourishing scale and the scale of positive and negative experience". *Social Indicators Research,* 118, 601–615.

Tambyah, S. K., & Tan, S. J. (2013). *Happiness and wellbeing: The Singaporean experience.* London: Routledge.

Tambyah, S. K., & Tan, S. J. (2018). *Happiness, wellbeing and society: What matters for Singaporeans.* London: Routledge.

Tinkler, L., & Hicks, S. (2011). *Measuring subjective well-being.* London: Office for National Statistics.

Veenhoven, R. (2012). "Happiness also known as 'life satisfaction' and 'subjective well-being'". In Kenneth C. Land, Alex C. Michalos, and M. Joseph Sirgy (Eds.), *Handbook of Social Indicators and Quality of Life Research* (pp. 63–77). Dordrecht, Netherlands: Springer Publishers.

Veroff, J., Douvan, E., & Kulka, R.A. (1981). *The inner American: A self-portrait from 1957 to 1976.* New York: Basic Books.

Villieux, A., Sovet, L., Jung, S-C., & Guilbert, L. (2016). "Psychological flourishing: validation of the French version of the flourishing scale and exploration of its relationships with personality traits". *Personality and Individual Differences, 88:*1–5.

4 The income-happiness equation for Singaporeans

Research studies on wellbeing have often examined the influence of various individual and societal factors on wellbeing outcomes. One of the more intriguing streams of research is centered on the question of whether having more income or money would make someone happier or more satisfied with their life. Numerous studies have examined this issue from diverse disciplinary perspectives, utilizing both extensive multicountry datasets and targeted country-specific datasets. In this chapter, we provide our contribution to the income-happiness debate using data from the 2022 QOL Survey and highlight several key issues that are pertinent to the Singaporean context.

To recap, for the 2022 QOL Survey, respondents were asked about their personal and household incomes. All respondents disclosed their personal income, unless they were unemployed, and all of them reported their household income. The income figures for this chapter are all in Singapore Dollars. For personal income, we had 1,554 data points from the weighted dataset, which were highly comparable to the national statistics on Singaporeans' gross monthly income, excluding the Central Provident Fund (CPF) contributions (Manpower Research and Statistics Department, Ministry of Manpower, 2023). The spread of personal income for the respondents in the 2022 QOL Survey was relatively similar to the distribution of Singaporeans' gross monthly income (Figure 4.1), with the national median personal income in 2022 ($4,083), inclusive of part time employment, falling within the median income bracket of the survey respondents ($4,000 to $4,999).

DOI: 10.4324/9781003399650-4

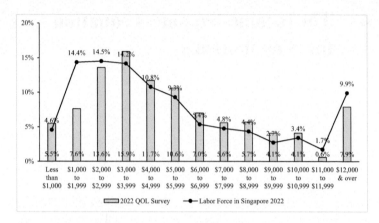

Figure 4.1 Distribution of personal income in 2022 QOL Survey and labor force in Singapore 2022 statistics.

Source: Manpower Research and Statistics Department, Ministry of Manpower (2023).

As data analyses using either household income or personal income yielded similar patterns of results, we decided to run the data analyses using household incomes for comparability across chapters. As mentioned earlier in this book, wellbeing outcomes encompass both affective aspects (such as happiness, and positive or negative affect) and cognitive aspects (such as life satisfaction). In the sections to follow, we discuss the relationship between household income and wellbeing outcomes such as happiness, enjoyment, achievement, control, purpose and satisfaction with life. We also have measures about perceptions of economic wellbeing and how satisfied respondents were about their life domains (e.g., household income and standard of living). We will examine if these related factors (such as financial satisfaction and satisfaction with standard of living) play a part in enhancing wellbeing.

Income and wellbeing outcomes

In general, research has shown that the influence of income depends on the aspect of wellbeing being measured. The effect of income on life satisfaction appeared to be stronger compared to positive and negative affect. For instance, having more money has been shown to improve the evaluations of one's life. It may also help to reduce daily sadness (negative affect) but not necessarily lead to more happiness (positive affect, Hudson et al., 2016; Kushlev et al., 2015; Sengupta et al., 2012). Using an extensive Gallup dataset, Diener et al. (2010) showed that national income (GDP per capita) had a positive effect on general life satisfaction but no effect on improvements in mood (i.e., the experience of positive or negative emotions). This suggested an important distinction between economic or material prosperity and psychosocial prosperity.

Geerling and Diener (2018) examined the relative strengths of societal characteristics, demographic variables and personal characteristics on life satisfaction, positive affect and negative affect among countries, and within the United States. They analyzed two sets of data: (1) the Gallup World Poll (2005 to 2015) consisting of 1.5 million adults across 166 nations, and (2) the Gallup-Sharecare 2015 Daily Survey consisting of 177,281 adults across all 50 states in the United States. They found that income had a strong effect on life satisfaction, but a small to medium effect on positive and negative affect.

Research on the effect of income on affective wellbeing yielded somewhat mixed results due to the wide range of emotions associated with positive and negative affect. Depending on the types of emotions that were examined, effect sizes had generally been smaller than the effect of income on life satisfaction. In a recent study that focused on emotions related to a sense of self-regard, Tong et al. (2021) found that income was a reliable predictor of greater positive self-regard emotions (such as pride, contentment and confidence) and lower negative self-regard emotions (anxiety, sadness, shame). However, the relationships between income and other self-regard emotions (gratitude and anger) and global emotions (happiness) were "unstable across studies, varying in magnitude and not highly replicable" (Tong et al., 2021, p. 1682). Additionally, they discovered that one's sense of control acted as a mediator of the relationships between both positive and negative self-regard emotions.

The relationship between income and happiness also varied for different levels of income. The income-wellbeing association was strongest for people earning below the median income and tended to plateau for those in the upper quartile. For instance, Drakopoulos and Grimani (2013) showed that there was a strong positive relationship between income and happiness for low-income households and a nonsignificant relationship between income and happiness for high-income households. In another study based on data from 24 countries between 2005 and 2013 in the Gallup World Poll and World Income Database, Powdthavee et al. (2017) explored the relationship between top-income earners and their wellbeing. Specifically, they discovered that top income earners reported lower average enjoyment and being well-rested and higher average stress and sadness.

Given the global effects of the COVID-19 pandemic between 2020 and 2022, researchers have taken the opportunity to study the effects of the pandemic on wellbeing. Using the survey results of 1,143 adults from RAND Corporation's nationally representative American Life Panel, Wanberg et al. (2020) conducted an analysis of changes in the psychological wellbeing of Americans before and during the COVID-19 pandemic, based on their socioeconomic status. The authors discovered that during the stated period of analysis, individuals who were top income earners experienced a greater decrease in life satisfaction in comparison with lower-income earners. This corroborated Geerling and Diener's (2018) findings that, contrary to intuition, higher income earners were not necessarily happier.

Why are rich nations and individuals not necessarily happier?

If income is posited to have a favorable impact on wellbeing outcomes, this seems to suggest that economic or material prosperity should be something that nations and individuals should strive for. However, researchers have found that higher absolute incomes (or actual incomes) do not necessarily lead to higher levels of happiness, a phenomenon that has been named "the Easterlin Paradox" (Easterlin, 1974). Although happiness and income often appeared to be positively related at the start, the association did not continue over time within a country. Rather, plateauing effects had often been observed. Easterlin et al. (2010) found this to be true for developing countries, transitioning countries in Eastern

Europe and a large sample of developed countries. A panel analysis conducted by Muresan et al. (2019) on a sample of 26 European countries demonstrated that happiness increased with individual annual income until a threshold of US$35,000.

One possible explanation is to take into account the effect of relative incomes because as long as basic needs have been met, social comparisons about incomes and the ability to meet higher order needs are prevalent in many societies (Diener & Oishi 2000; Diener & Seligman, 2009; Drakopoulos, 2013; Oshio & Urakawa, 2014). Studies have found that relative incomes and income aspirations were significantly correlated to wellbeing (e.g., Knight & Gunatilaka, 2011), and even more so for East Asian countries such as China, Japan, and South Korea (Huang et al., 2016; Yamashita et al., 2016). Social comparisons operate at various levels and within different comparison or reference groups (e.g., with those who work in the same occupation and those who live in the same region). Some studies have used perceived social class (Guven & Sorensen, 2012) or the ranked position of someone's income within a comparison group (Boyce et al., 2010). Through an analysis of the British Household Panel Survey and Understanding Society data from 1996 to 2017, FitzRoy and Nolan (2021) found that ranked income, absolute income and relative income were all significant variables that affected life satisfaction and happiness.

Using data from the Canadian National Population Health Survey (1994 to 2009), Latif (2016) found that an increase in the average income of the reference group reduced individual happiness. An individual was happier when his/her own household income grew compared to the average income of the reference group, even for different reference groups. In short, comparison income had a significant negative impact on an individual's happiness level. This finding was supported by Ugur's (2021) study on individuals in Turkey. Similar to Latif (2016), Ugur's (2021) analysis of 300,000 data responses from a Life Satisfaction Survey (2003 to 2017) revealed that relative income mattered more than absolute income for happiness. Specifically, when there was an increase in the average income of the city in which a person resided in, the level of happiness was reduced substantially leading to an offset of the happiness effect of an increase in absolute income.

This effect of relative income on happiness was also found to affect men more than women in Turkey.

In an analysis of 2008 to 2009 data from 11,791 individuals across 32 cities in the People's Republic of China, Li et al. (2022) demonstrated that that an individual's absolute income had significant predictive effects on relative income and wellbeing, with relative income playing a mediating role on the association between absolute income and wellbeing. Additionally, GDP was found to be a moderator for two relationships. Firstly, in cities with higher levels of GDP, the effect of absolute income on wellbeing was stronger. Secondly, in cities with lower levels of GDP, the relationship between absolute income and relative income was stronger.

Household income and wellbeing outcomes for Singaporeans

In the following sections, we first examine the associations between household income and the affective aspects of wellbeing (i.e., happiness, enjoyment, achievement, control and purpose). Then we investigate how the cognitive aspect of wellbeing varied with income.

Household income and affective aspects of wellbeing

Respondents in the 2022 QOL Survey initially answered the question on happiness "All things considered, would you say that you are happy these days?" with a five-point scale of "1 = Very unhappy" to "5 = Very happy". However, for consistency in analyses, we recoded the responses to a four-point scale for parity with the questions on enjoyment, achievement, control and purpose. The recoding was done as follows: 1 and 2 were recoded as 1 = Unhappy, 3 was recoded as 2 = Neither Happy nor Unhappy, 4 was recoded as 3 = Quite Happy, and 5 was recoded as 4 = Very Happy. The question on enjoyment ("How often do you feel you are really enjoying life these days?") had a four-point scale of "1 = Never" to "4 = Often", and the question on achievement ("How much do you feel you are accomplishing what you want out of life?") also had a four-point scale of "1 = None" to "4 = A great deal". Respondents replied to the question on control of "How much control do you feel you have over important aspects of your life?"), and the question on sense of purpose ("All things considered, how much do you feel you have a sense of purpose in your life?") with a four-point scale of "1 = None" to "4 = A great deal".

As shown in Figure 4.2, Singaporeans' levels of happiness, enjoyment, and achievement increased linearly with household

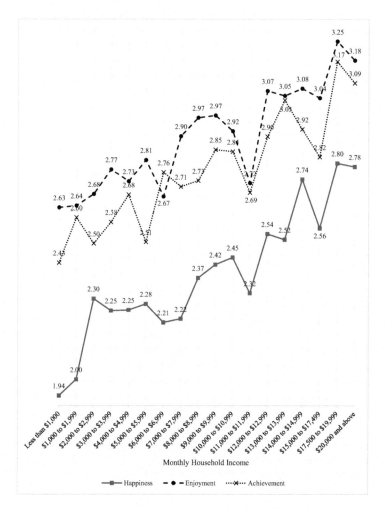

Figure 4.2 Happiness, enjoyment and achievement across household income levels (2022).

income. Specifically, for happiness (solid gray line), there was a sharp increase for the $2,000 to $2,999 income bracket. The incremental slope featured plateaus at different junctures. For instance, respondents earning $3,000 to $5,999 had similar means from 2.25 to 2.28. Respondents earning $12,000 to $13,999 had means hovering around 2.52 to 2.54. Happiness remained fairly constant for those whose monthly household income fell in the range of $3,000 to $7,999. Happiness took a sharp dip for those with monthly household incomes of $11,000 to $11,999 and $15,000 to $17,499. Singaporeans with the lowest household income (< $1,000) reported the lowest happiness level, while those who earned between $17,500 and $19,999 had the highest level of happiness.

While Singaporeans with higher household incomes tended to have greater enjoyment and achievement, we observed more acute ebb and flow in the associations between income and enjoyment (dashed line) and between income and achievement achievement (dotted line). Those earning $4,000 to $4,999 reported similar levels of enjoyment as those earning $11,000 to $11,999. For the income bracket of $6,000 to $6,999, the enjoyment score (2.67) appeared to be similar to the three lowest income brackets (means ranging from 2.63 to 2.68). There was even more variability for achievement, which made it difficult to note patterns in the associations. Like what was noted for happiness, those with the lowest income (< $1,000) reported the lowest levels of enjoyment and achievement, while Singaporeans with a household income of between $17,500 and $19,999 had the greatest enjoyment and achievement.

The relations between household income with Singaporeans' sense of control (solid gray line) and purpose (dashed line) in life are presented in Figure 4.3. Control and purpose appeared to be closely correlated. Similar to happiness, enjoyment and achievement, Singaporeans' sense of control and purpose also increased with higher household income. However, there could be exceptions where Singaporeans in a higher income group ($20,000 and above) reported fairly similar scores for control as those earning $13,000 to $14,999. Once again, the group with the lowest income (< $1,000) had the lowest control and purpose, and the group that earns between $17,500 and $19,999 scored the highest on the two indices.

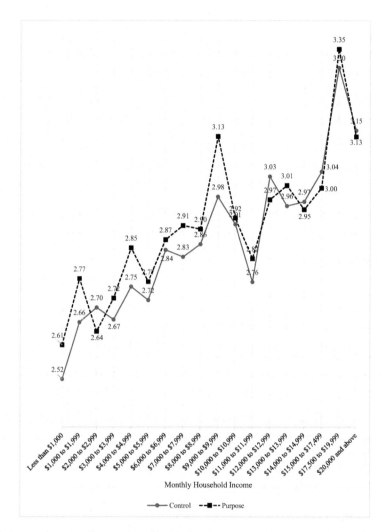

Figure 4.3 Control and sense of purpose across household income levels (2022).

Household income and cognitive aspects of wellbeing

The cognitive aspects of wellbeing were evaluated with the 5-item Satisfaction with Life scale and a single question assessing Singaporeans' satisfaction with their overall quality of life. The five statements (1 = "Strongly disagree", 6 = "Strongly agree") about satisfaction with life include, "In most ways, my life is close to my ideal", "The conditions of my life are excellent", "I am satisfied with my life", "So far I have gotten the important things I want in life" and "If I could live my life over, I would change almost nothing". Each respondent's responses to the five items were averaged and used to compare with their household income. The single-item measure on the overall quality of life asked participants to rate their satisfaction with their "overall quality of life in general" on a six-point scale (1 = "Very dissatisfied", 6 = "Very satisfied"). Higher scores on either measure indicated better cognitive wellbeing.

As shown in Figure 4.4, the two measures of cognitive wellbeing followed highly similar trends. Both satisfaction with life (dark gray line) and satisfaction with the overall quality of life (dashed line) increased linearly with higher household income. The first notable inflection point for both satisfaction with life and satisfaction with the overall quality of life occurred when the satisfaction levels dropped sharply for those with household income between $5,000 and $5,999. Satisfaction levels continued to rise as income increased until they reached another peak among Singaporeans with income between $13,000 and $13,999, and then dipped for the next two income brackets. Finally, satisfaction with life and satisfaction with the overall quality of life rebounded and reached the highest point among Singaporeans who earned between $17,500 and $19,999. The pattern of results for cognitive wellbeing was comparable to the affective aspects of wellbeing, whereby Singaporeans with the lowest income (< $1,000) had the poorest wellbeing, and those earning $17,500 to $19,999 reporting the highest wellbeing.

In addition to Figures 4.2 to 4.4, we examined correlations between household income and the wellbeing outcomes. The correlations were all positive and ranged from 0.173 to 0.244, indicating that household income had an influence on Singaporeans' wellbeing (see Table 4.1).

We also examined related concepts such as financial satisfaction (i.e., how satisfied one is with the financial situation of their

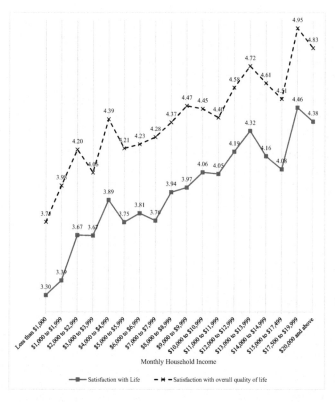

Figure 4.4 Satisfaction with life and satisfaction with overall QOL across household income levels (2022).

Table 4.1 Correlations between wellbeing outcomes and household incomes (2022)

Wellbeing Outcomes	*Household Income*
Happiness	0.219***
Enjoyment	0.202***
Achievement	0.226**
Control	0.208***
Sense of purpose	0.173***
Satisfaction with Life	0.244***
Satisfaction with overall quality of life	0.217***

Note: *** correlation is significant at 0.001 level.

Table 4.2 Correlations between satisfaction with household income and standard of living with wellbeing outcomes (2022)

Wellbeing Outcomes	Satisfaction with Household Income	Satisfaction with Standard of Living
Happiness	0.492[***]	0.505[***]
Enjoyment	0.467[***]	0.489[***]
Achievement	0.484[***]	0.520[***]
Control	0.443[***]	0.474[***]
Sense of purpose	0.448[***]	0.464[***]
Satisfaction with Life	0.636[***]	0.641[***]
Satisfaction with overall quality of life	0.661[***]	0.717[***]

Note: [***] correlation is significant at 0.001 level.

household) and satisfaction with standard of living. Similar to Ng et al. (2017), our correlation analyses confirmed that satisfaction with household incomes (i.e., financial satisfaction) and satisfaction with standard of living were positively associated with the wellbeing outcomes (see Table 4.2).

Economic wellbeing

The impact of income on happiness can also be assessed with indicators of economic wellbeing (as shown in Figure 4.5). In 2022, about three quarters (78.3 per cent) of Singaporeans agreed that they have enough money to buy the things they need, compared to 83.9 per cent in 2016. The percentage of Singaporeans who were able to repay their monthly loans rose slightly from 72.5 per cent in 2016 to 77.2 per cent in 2022. The percentage of Singaporeans who have enough money to do what they want also increased slightly from 61.4 per cent in 2016 to 63.8 per cent in 2022. Almost two thirds (60.0 per cent) of Singaporeans reported that they were able to make major purchases in 2022, compared to slightly more than one third (44.6 per cent) in 2016.

Sources of individual differences for economic wellbeing

Sources of individual differences for economic wellbeing are shown in Table 4.3. Singaporeans' economic wellbeing did not

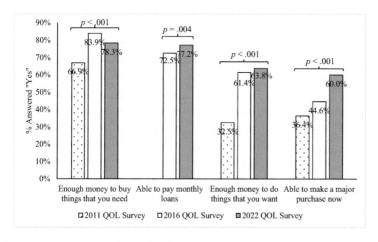

Figure 4.5 Indicators of economic wellbeing for 2011, 2016 and 2022 QOL Surveys.

vary by gender, although it does help if Singaporeans are married, probably with the pooling of resources, compared to singles with only one income. Married Singaporeans fared better in being able to pay monthly loans (72.4 per cent for singles versus 80 per cent for married Singaporeans), in having enough money to do what they want (58.7 per cent for singles versus 66.9 per cent for married Singaporeans), and in being able to make a major purchase (52.8 per cent for singles versus 64.4 per cent for married Singaporeans).

Older Singaporeans were significantly better off than their younger counterparts. More than eight out of ten Singaporeans aged 60 years and above (87.8 per cent for 60–69 years and 83.8 per cent for 70–79 years) reported that they were able to have enough money to buy things they need and to pay their monthly loans. This compared favorably against younger Singaporeans, like those in the 40 to 49 years age group, where seven out of ten (73.7 per cent) agreed they have enough money to buy things they need, or those in the 20 to 29 years age group, where only seven out of ten (72.9 per cent) were able to pay their monthly loans.

Singaporeans' economic wellbeing also improved significantly as their level of education increased. For instance, while six out of

Table 4.3 Sources of individual differences for economic wellbeing (2022)

Demographics	Enough money to buy things that you need	Able to pay monthly loans	Enough money to do things that you want	Able to make a major purchase now
Gender				
- Male	77.8%	77.7%	65.9%	63.2%
- Female	78.8%	76.7%	61.8%	57.0%
- Chi-square	0.26	0.26	3.01	6.91
- *p*	0.610	0.607	0.083	0.009
Marital Status				
- Single	78.3%	72.4%	58.7%	52.8%
- Married	78.3%	80.0%	66.9%	64.4%
- Chi-square	0.00	12.87	11.67	22.40
- *p*	0.995	< 0.001	< 0.001	< 0.001
Age				
- 20–29	79.9%	72.4%	63.4%	61.3%
- 30–39	74.1%	76.7%	63.4%	65.5%
- 40–49	73.7%	72.9%	61.5%	60.5%
- 50–59	76.4%	76.9%	61.8%	58.6%
- 60–69	87.8%	84.6%	67.4%	52.5%
- 70–79	83.8%	92.7%	75.5%	65.6%
- Chi-square	27.14	24.64	6.73	12.67
- *p*	< 0.001	< 0.001	0.241	0.027
Education				
- Low	65.9%	63.4%	50.3%	43.7%
- Medium	75.9%	75.4%	59.6%	55.8%
- High	83.5%	82.5%	70.0%	67.3%
- Chi-square	47.44	50.22	44.68	60.12
- *p*	< 0.001	< 0.001	< 0.001	< 0.001
Household Income				
- Low	61.4%	56.4%	42.8%	34.7%
- Medium-low	72.8%	69.7%	50.2%	45.2%
- Medium-high	84.5%	84.9%	74.2%	71.4%
- High	89.6%	91.0%	85.7%	85.9%
- Chi-square	84.56	121.34	173.11	219.08
- *p*	< 0.001	< 0.001	< 0.001	< 0.001

ten with low education (65.9 per cent) reported they have enough money to buy things, eight out of ten (83.5 per cent) with high education levels were able to do so. The difference is more notice-able when it involves having enough money to do what you want. Five out of 10 (50.3 per cent) of Singaporeans with low education reported they were able to do so, while seven out of ten (70 per cent) Singaporeans with high education could do so. Also, when it involves being able to make a major purchase, four out of ten (43.7 per cent) of Singaporeans with low education reported they were able to do so, compared with more than six out of ten (67.5 per cent) Singaporeans with high education.

Since income is positively correlated with education levels in Singapore, Singaporeans' economic wellbeing improved sig-nificantly as household income increased. For instance, when it involves having enough money to do what you want, four out of ten (42.8 per cent) of Singaporeans with low household income reported they were able to do so, compared with eight out of ten (84.9 per cent) Singaporeans with medium-high household income and nine out of ten (91 per cent) for those with high household income. Three out of ten (34.7 per cent) of Singaporeans with low household income reported they were able to make a major pur-chase, compared with seven out of ten (71.4 per cent) and eight out of ten (85.9 per cent) Singaporeans with medium-high and high household incomes, respectively.

Conclusion

Our data analyses revealed some interesting trends between house-hold income and wellbeing outcomes. However, as some income brackets had smaller numbers of respondents, these observations should be taken with a note of caution and they do not suggest any causality. Happiness seemed to increase as household incomes increased. There were exceptions where Singaporeans in a higher income group ($11,000 to $11,999) may not be happier than those in the lower income groups ($10,000 to $10,999). In terms of the level of enjoyment, although Singaporeans who did not enjoy life as much were primarily from the lower income groups, enjoyment levels for those in the middle-income groups ($7,001 to $10,999) were not much lower than those earning $12,000 to $17,999. Although household income had a positive relationship with

Singaporeans' sense of achievement, there were again exceptions where people with higher income ($15,000 to $17,499) reported lower levels of achievement than those in lower income brackets ($12,000 to $14,999).

Income does matter in Singaporeans' level of control over important aspects of their life, and their sense of purpose, both of which generally improved as income increased but there were again exceptions. For instance, those earning $9,000 to $9,999 reported fairly similar scores for control as those earning $13,000 to $14,999, and similar scores for purpose as those earning twice as much ($20,000 and above).

Income also had a positive relationship with Singaporeans' satisfaction with life and their overall quality of life. Both satisfaction measures seemed to be rather closely correlated and several similar peaks were noted in the graphs as well, with the highest peak noted for those earning $17,500 to $19,999. There was a slight dip for the $14,000 to $17,999 income brackets.

How are Singaporeans doing in terms of economic wellbeing? In 2022, the percentage of Singaporeans (78.3 per cent) who agreed that they had enough money to buy the things they need fell compared to 83.9 per cent in 2016. Conversely, the percentages of Singaporeans who were able to repay their monthly loans increased from 72.5 per cent in 2016 to 77.2 per cent in 2022. Similarly, the percentage of Singaporeans who had enough money to do what they want also improved slightly from 61.4 per cent in 2016 to 63.8 percent in 2022. The largest improvement was noted for 60 per cent of Singaporeans who reported that they were able to make major purchases in 2022, compared to slightly more than one third (44.6 per cent) in 2016. Singaporeans who were married and with higher levels of education and household incomes generally found it easier to cope with their needs, monthly loans, wants and major purchases. There were no age differences for wants and major purchases, but younger Singaporeans reported that they did not have enough for their needs and monthly loans.

References

Boyce, C. J., Brown, G. D. A., & Moore, S. C. (2010). "Money and happiness". *Psychological Science*, *21*(4), 471–475. https://doi.org/10.1177/0956797610362671

Diener, E., & Oishi, S. (2000). "Money and happiness: Income and subjective well-being across nations". In E. Diener & E. Suh (Eds.), *Culture and subjective well-being* (pp. 185–218). Cambridge, MA: The MIT Press.

Diener, E., & Seligman, M. P. (2009). "Beyond money: Toward an economy of wellbeing". In E. Diener (Ed.), *The science of wellbeing* (vol. 37, pp. 201–265). Netherlands: Springer.

Diener, E., Ng, W., Harter, J., & Arora, R. (2010). "Wealth and happiness across the world: Material prosperity predicts life evaluation, whereas psychosocial prosperity predicts positive feeling". *Journal of Personality and Social Psychology*, *99*(1), 52–61.

Drakopoulos, S.A. (2013). "Hierarchical needs, income comparisons, and happiness levels". In A. Efklides & D. Moraitou (Eds.), *A positive psychology perspective on quality of life* (pp. 17–32). New York: Springer Science + Business Media.

Drakopoulos, S.A., & Grimani, K. (2013). "Maslow's needs hierarchy and the effect of income on happiness levels". In F. Sarracino (Ed.), *The happiness compass: Theories, actions and perspectives for well-being* (pp. 295–309). Hauppauge, NY: Nova Science Publishers.

Easterlin, R.A. (1974). *Does economic growth improve the human lot? Some empirical evidence in nations and households in economic growth.* New York: Academic Press

Easterlin, R.A., McVey, L.A., Switek, M, Sawangfa, O., & Zweig, J.S. (2010). "The happiness-income paradox revisited". *Proceedings of the National Academy of Sciences*, *107*(52), 22243–22468.

FitzRoy, F. R., & Nolan, M. A. (2021). "Income status and life satisfaction". *Journal of Happiness Studies*, *23*(1), 233–256. https://doi.org/10.1007/s10902-021-00397-y

Geerling, D. M., & Diener, E. (2018). "Effect size strengths in subjective well-being research". *Applied Research in Quality of Life*, *15*(1), 167–185. https://doi.org/10.1007/s11482-018-9670-8

Guven, C., & Sorensen, B. E. (2012). "Subjective wellbeing: Keeping up with the perception of the Joneses". *Social Indicators Research*, *109*, 439–469.

Huang, J., Wu, S., & Deng, S. (2016). "Relative income, relative assets, and happiness in urban China". *Social Indicators Research*, *126*, 971–985.

Hudson, N. W., Lucas, R. E., Donnellan, M. B., & Kushlev, K. (2016). "Income reliably predicts daily sadness, but not happiness, A replication and extension of Kushlev, Dunn, and Lucas (2015)". *Social Psychological and Personality Science*, *7*, 828–836.

Knight, J., & Gunatilaka, R. (2011). "'Great expectations?' The subjective wellbeing of rural-urban migrants in China". *Oxford Development Studies, 39*(1), 1–24.

Kushlev, K., Dunn, E. W., & Lucas, R. E. (2015). "Higher income is associated with less daily sadness but not more daily happiness". *Social Psychological and Personality Science*, 6, 483–489.

Latif, E. (2016). "Happiness and comparison income: Evidence from Canada". *Social Indicators Research*, 128, 161–177.

Li, F., Mu, W., Li, S., Li, X., Zhang, J., Chen, C., & Zhou, M. J. (2022). "Income and subjective well-being: Test of a multilevel moderated mediation model". *Applied Research in Quality of Life*, 17(4), 2041–2058. https://doi.org/10.1007/s11482-021-10017-9

Manpower Research and Statistics Department, Ministry of Manpower. (2023). *Labour Force in Singapore 2022 Edition.* https://stats.mom.gov.sg/Pages/Labour-Force-in-Singapore-2022.aspx

Muresan, G. M., Ciumas, C., & Achim, M. V. (2019). "Can money buy happiness? Evidence for European countries". *Applied Research in Quality of Life*, 15(4), 953–970. https://doi.org/10.1007/s11482-019-09714-3

Ng, W., Kua, W. S. R., & Kang, S. (2019). "The relative importance of personality, financial satisfaction, and autonomy for different subjective well-being facets". *The Journal of Psychology*, 153(7), 680–700. https://doi.org/10.1080/00223980.2019.1598928

Oshio, T., & Urakawa, K. (2014). "The association between perceived income inequality and subjective wellbeing: Evidence from a social survey in Japan". *Social Indicators Research*, 116, 755–770.

Powdthavee, N. Burkhauser, R. V. and De Neve, J. (2017). "Top incomes and human well-being: Evidence from the Gallup World Poll". *Journal of Economic Psychology*, 62, 246–257.

Sengupta, N. K., Osborne, D., Houkamau, C. A., Hoverd, W.J., Wilson, M. S., & Halliday, L. M. (2012). "How much happiness does money buy? Income and subjective well-being in New Zealand". *New Zealand Journal of Psychology*, 41(2), 21–34.

Tong, E. M., Reddish, P., Oh, V. Y., Ng, W., Sasaki, E., Chin, E. D., & Diener, E. (2022). "Income robustly predicts self-regard emotions". *Emotion*, 22(7), 1670–1685. https://doi.org/10.1037/emo0000933

Ugur, Z. B. (2021). "How does inequality hamper subjective well-being? The role of fairness". *Social Indicators Research*, 158(2), 377–407. https://doi.org/10.1007/s11205-021-02711-w

Wanberg, C. R., Csillag, B., Douglass, R. P., Zhou, L., & Pollard, M. S. (2020). "Socioeconomic status and well-being during COVID-19: A resource-based examination". *Journal of Applied Psychology*, 105(12), 1382–1396. https://doi.org/10.1037/apl0000831

Yamashita, T. Bardo, A., & Liu, D. (2016). "Are East Asians happy to work more or less? Associations between working hours, relative income and happiness in China, Japan, South Korea and Taiwan". *Asian Journal of Social Psychology*, 19, 264–274.

5 Values and their influence on Singaporeans' wellbeing

Values and their impact on behaviors and wellbeing outcomes have been a fruitful area of research in the social sciences (e.g., Rokeach, 1968; 1973). Values can be defined as "the whole constellation of a person's attitudes, beliefs, opinions, hopes, fears, prejudices, needs, desires, and aspirations that, taken together, govern how one behaves" (Mitchell, 1983). Values premised on religious beliefs also have a significant influence on individuals and communities.

Many country- and region-level studies (e.g., European Social Survey and our QOL Surveys in Singapore) have incorporated measures on values. One of the largest studies is the World Values Survey (WVS), a global network of social scientists that has been studying changing values and their impact on social and political life since 1981. Publications using the WVS have contributed substantially to our understanding of how value systems influence various aspects of our lives. The questionnaires for these surveys cover a diverse range of issues such as "cultural values, attitudes and beliefs towards gender, family, and religion, attitudes and experience of poverty, education, health, and security, social tolerance and trust, attitudes towards multilateral institutions, cultural differences and similarities between regions and societies" and topics such as "justice, moral principles, corruption, accountability and risk, migration, national security and global governance". Other measures have also been conceptualized and developed. For example, the List of Values (LOV, Kahle, 1983, 1996), consisting of nine personal values, has been used in many contexts and has well-documented reliability and validity (Stockard et al., 2014).

DOI: 10.4324/9781003399650-5

Another established measure is the Portrait Values Questionnaire (Schwartz, 2007), which we used in the 2016 QOL Survey.

In this chapter, we use the LOV to assess the importance of certain personal values to Singaporeans and provide additional analyses by gender, marital status, age, education and household income. In addition to tracking changes in the LOV over time, we will examine the impact of the LOV values on Singaporeans' wellbeing. Depending on the availability of data, we provide some comparisons to the WVS Wave 7 (2017–2022).

List of values

In this section, we examine how Singaporeans felt about some personal values using the LOV. There are nine items in this measure, namely: (1) sense of belonging; (2) excitement; (3) fun and enjoyment in life; (4) warm relationships with others; (5) self-fulfillment; (6) being well-respected; (7) sense of accomplishment; (8) security and (9) self-respect (see Table 5.1).

Among the nine values, we expect Singaporeans to place the least emphasis on Excitement and Fun and Enjoyment in Life. The World Values Survey conducted by the Institute of Policy

Table 5.1 List of values

Value	Description
Sense of Belonging	To be accepted and needed by your family, friends and community.
Security	To be safe and protected from misfortune and attack.
Self-respect	To be proud of yourself and confident with who you are.
Warm Relationships with Others	To have close companionships and intimate friendships.
Fun and Enjoyment in Life	To lead a pleasurable life.
Being Well-respected	To be admired by others and to receive recognition.
Sense of Accomplishment	To succeed at whatever you do.
Self-fulfillment	To find peace of mind and to make the best use of your talents.
Excitement	To experience stimulation and thrills.

Source: Kahle (1996).

Studies (IPS) from November 2019 to March 2020 on over 2000 Singaporeans found leisure to be among the four lowest priorities (Elangovan, 2021). Similar to other countries in Asia, according to the WVS 2017–2022, only half of those in China (50 per cent) and less than half of those in Japan (45.8 per cent) agreed that leisure is important. By comparison, in South Korea, a majority (67.5 per cent) rated leisure time as "Rather Important". Among ASEAN countries, only Indonesia had a majority (50.4 per cent) reporting that Leisure time is "Very Important" while the majority of Malaysians, Singaporeans and Thais reported leisure time as only "Rather Important" (48 per cent, 55.8 percent and 49.8 per cent, for Malaysia, Singapore and Thailand, respectively, Haerpfer et al., 2022). In their study of changes in social values in the United States over 30 years from 1976 to 2007, Gurel-Atay et al. (2010) found that values such as self-respect and fun-enjoyment-excitement showed the greatest gain in importance, with self-respect being the most important value in 2007. Warm relationships with others and self-fulfillment were close seconds in order of importance. The values of security and sense of belonging demonstrated the most decline in importance. They also found that there was a reverse pattern in importance placed on different values; more important values in 1986 were perceived as being less important in 2007.

In Singapore, the LOV has been used in nationwide surveys conducted in 1996, 2001, 2011, 2016 and 2022. In all five surveys, respondents were asked to rate the nine values in the LOV on a six-point scale (1 = Not important at all; 6 = Very important). The mean score of each value was used to rank the values from the most important to the least.

General comparisons for choices and ranks

In Figure 5.1, we report the percentages of respondents who picked a particular value as "important" or "very important". As shown in the figure, the choice of important values changed over the years, with a definitive negative trend for all nine values, especially when compared to the 2011 and 2016 QOL Surveys. All except two values (security and sense of belonging) showed new low levels of importance compared to previous years. The steepest decline was for the value of being well-respected, which declined from 71.7 per

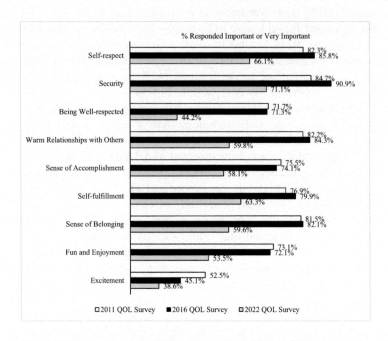

Figure 5.1 Importance of different values from 2011 to 2022.

cent in 2011 to 44.2 per cent in 2022. The next steep decline was observed for the value of warm relationships with others, which declined from a high of 84.3 per cent in 2016 to a new low of 59.8 per cent, followed by the value of sense of belonging, which declined from a high of 82.1 per cent in 2016 to a low of 59.6 per cent in 2022. The value of security also declined in importance from a high of 90.9 per cent in 2016 to a low of 71.1 per cent in 2022, and the value of self-respect declined from a high of 85.8 per cent in 2016 to a new low of 66.1 per cent in 2022. The values of sense of accomplishment, self-fulfillment, fun and enjoyment and excitement also reported new low levels of importance. Sense of accomplishment fell in importance from a high of 74.1 per cent in 2016 to a new low of 58.1 per cent in 2022, self-fulfillment fell in importance from a high of 79.9 per cent in 2016 to a new low of 63.3 per cent in 2022, fun and enjoyment fell in importance from a high of 73.1 per cent in 2016 to a new low of 53.5 per cent in 2022 and excitement fell from 45.3 per cent in 2016 to a new low of 38.6 per cent in 2022.

Apart from the significant declining trend observed in the importance levels of the values over the years, the ranking of the importance means for the values revealed some interesting insights (see Table 5.2). In 2011, security was the most important value, followed by self-respect and warm relationships with others. Being well-respected ranked 7th out of nine values. Five years later in 2016, the top two values remained the same as those in 2011 but being well-respected declined to being ranked 8th out of nine values. Another six years later, the top two values remained the same as those in 2016, but self-fulfillment became the third most important factor, replacing warm relationships with others. Meanwhile, being well-respected continued to remain less important, being ranked 8th out of nine values. Some consistency was also being observed in Singaporeans' views of the importance of the nine values, with fun and enjoyment being ranked either 7th or 8th, and excitement was always ranked last over the last three editions of QOL Surveys. The low importance accorded to fun and enjoyment is consistent with the findings of the WVS conducted by IPS (Elangovan, 2021).

Table 5.2 List of values (ranking of importance means) for 2011, 2016 and 2022

List of Values	2022 (rank)	2016 (rank)	2011 (rank)
Security	4.94 (1)	5.19 (1)	5.09 (1)
Self-respect	4.80 (2)	5.06 (2)	5.03 (2)
Self-fulfillment	4.77 (3)	4.93 (5)	4.93 (5)
Warm Relationships with Others	4.67 (4)	5.02 (3)	4.99 (3)
Sense of Belonging	4.64 (5)	4.97 (4)	4.98 (4)
Sense of Accomplishment	4.63 (6)	4.82 (6)	4.90 (6)
Fun and Enjoyment	4.55 (7)	4.80 (7)	4.85 (8)
Being Well-respected	4.26 (8)	4.75 (8)	4.88 (7)
Excitement	4.13 (9)	4.14 (9)	4.44 (9)

Note: Means of scale ranging from 1=Not important at all to 6=Very important.

Sources of individual differences in LOV

Gender

Female Singaporeans tended to hold values such as self-respect, security (Table 5.3a), and self-fulfillment (Table 5.3b) as being more important than male Singaporeans. Conversely, males valued excitement more than females. We have not found any extant studies that examined gender differences in the LOV.

Marital Status

Married Singaporeans valued being well-respected (Table 5.3a) and sense of belonging (Table 5.3b) more than their single counterparts. Although we did not find significant differences for fun and enjoyment between married versus single Singaporeans, a WVS conducted by IPS from November 2019 to March 2020 on over 2,000 Singaporeans found that "Nearly 40 per cent of singles rated leisure time as very important, compared to less than 30 per cent of married respondents" (Elangovan, 2021). We have not found any extant studies that examined differences in the LOV for marital status.

Age

As shown in the third column of Table 5.3a, age had a U-shaped and significant pattern with the value of being well-respected: Singaporeans in the 50 to 59 and 60 to 69 years old age groups regarded this value to be less important compared to their younger and older compatriots. However, age showed a signifi-cant and linear declining trend for the values of sense of accom-plishment, fun and enjoyment, and excitement (Table 5.3b). In other words, older Singaporeans tended to place less importance on these three values, as compared to younger ones. This trend is also supported by the findings of the same IPS study mentioned earlier: "About 40 per cent of those aged between 21 and 35 said leisure time was very important, compared to about 20 per cent of those above 65" (Elangovan, 2021).

Our results about older Singaporeans contrasted with findings from research on LOV of older persons in other parts of the world, some of which examined both chronological age, as well as cognitive or self-perceived age. For instance, in a study involving

356 Australian seniors in age ranging between 56 and 93 years, Cleaver and Muller (2002) found that those who had younger self-perceived age placed more importance on fun and enjoyment, while those who had older self-perceived age placed greater importance on security.

In a study involving 650 older consumers (above 50 years of age) in the United Kingdom, Sudbury and Simcock (2009) found that the most important value to the older consumers was self-respect, followed by security, warm relationships with others and a sense of accomplishment, with being well-respected as the least important value. However, in terms of self-reported cognitive age, Sudhury and Simcock (2009) found that while self-respect was of greatest importance to the older cognitive age groups (40s, 50s and 60s), the youngest cognitive age group (30s) placed the greatest importance on warm relationships with others. Strong negative correlations were found between cognitive age and warm relationships with others, fun and enjoyment and self-fulfillment. Strong positive correlations were found between cognitive age and security, sense of accomplishment, and sense of belonging.

Education

Education had an unanimously positive and significant correlation with the values of self-respect, security, being well-respected and warm relationships with others (Table 5.3a) and all five values of sense of accomplishment, self-fulfillment, sense of belonging, fun and enjoyment, as well as excitement in Table 5.3b. The more educated Singaporeans were, the more they endorsed each of the nine values. We have not found any extant studies that examined differences between the LOV and education.

Household income

Similar to education, household income also had strong effects on Singaporeans' endorsement of the nine values. Household income had a positive and significant correlation with the values of self-respect, security, being well-respected and warm relationships with others (Table 5.3a) and all five values of sense of accomplishment, self-fulfillment, sense of belonging, fun and enjoyment, as well as excitement, as seen in Table 5.3b. The positive relationship

Table 5.3a Sources of individual differences in importance for self-respect, security, being well-respected and warm relationships with others (2022)

Demographics	Self-Respect	Security	Being Well-respected	Warm Relationships with Others
Gender				
- Male	4.71	4.82	4.26	4.63
- Female	4.89	5.06	4.26	4.71
- *F*-Stats	14.77	23.07	0.00	2.90
- *p*	< 0.001	< 0.001	0.990	0.089
Marital Status				
- Single	4.81	4.89	4.15	4.65
- Married	4.80	4.98	4.33	4.68
- *F*-Stats	0.14	3.26	9.79	0.40
- *p*	0.707	0.071	0.002	0.529
Age				
- 20–29	4.85	4.87	4.46	4.76
- 30–39	4.88	4.93	4.46	4.69
- 40–49	4.80	4.89	4.30	4.69
- 50–59	4.78	5.06	4.01	4.58
- 60–69	4.72	4.99	4.03	4.64
- 70–79	4.68	4.79	4.35	4.62
- *F*-Stats	1.28	1.91	9.78	1.16
- *p*	0.268	0.090	< 0.001	0.329
Education				
- Low	4.68	4.81	4.03	4.52
- Medium	4.74	4.91	4.14	4.60
- High	4.87	5.00	4.39	4.75
- *F*-Stats	5.90	5.19	14.83	7.65
- *p*	0.003	0.006	< 0.001	< 0.001
Household Income				
- Low	4.69	4.81	3.90	4.48
- Medium-low	4.80	4.92	4.22	4.64
- Medium-high	4.77	4.96	4.35	4.71
- High	4.99	5.09	4.45	4.81
- *F*-Stats	4.84	3.61	11.88	4.89
- *p*	0.002	0.013	< 0.001	0.002

Table 5.3b Sources of individual differences in importance for sense of accomplishment, self-fulfillment, sense of belonging, fun and enjoyment and excitement (2022)

Demographics	Sense of Accomplishment	Self-Fulfillment	Sense of Belonging	Fun and Enjoyment	Excitement
Gender					
- Male	4.62	4.71	4.59	4.50	4.20
- Female	4.64	4.84	4.69	4.60	4.07
- F-Stats	0.15	7.87	3.90	4.09	5.09
- p	0.700	0.005	0.048	0.043	0.024
Marital Status					
- Single	4.58	4.76	4.54	4.53	4.08
- Married	4.65	4.78	4.70	4.57	4.17
- F-Stats	2.09	0.09	9.70	0.59	2.13
- p	0.149	0.770	0.002	0.441	0.145
Age					
- 20–29	4.74	4.77	4.69	4.76	4.46
- 30–39	4.71	4.87	4.65	4.73	4.49
- 40–49	4.59	4.77	4.62	4.54	4.19
- 50–59	4.53	4.73	4.66	4.46	3.90
- 60–69	4.56	4.74	4.58	4.37	3.75
- 70–79	4.68	4.74	4.71	4.09	3.56
- F-Stats	2.42	0.85	0.41	10.80	26.19
- p	0.034	0.517	0.839	< 0.001	< 0.001

(*Continued*)

Table 5.3b (Continued)

Demographics	Sense of Accomplishment	Self-Fulfillment	Sense of Belonging	Fun and Enjoyment	Excitement
Education					
- Low	4.49	4.61	4.46	4.40	3.87
- Medium	4.54	4.70	4.65	4.51	3.98
- High	4.71	4.86	4.70	4.62	4.29
- F-Stats	8.34	9.78	6.95	6.92	22.22
- p	< 0.001	< 0.001	< 0.001	0.001	< 0.001
Household Income					
- Low	4.42	4.61	4.44	4.24	3.81
- Medium-low	4.57	4.73	4.62	4.53	4.04
- Medium-high	4.63	4.78	4.65	4.60	4.20
- High	4.92	5.01	4.87	4.78	4.49
- F-Stats	12.31	8.01	7.50	12.85	17.06
- p	< 0.001	< 0.001	< 0.001	< 0.001	< 0.001

between income and fun and enjoyment is also mentioned in the earlier mentioned IPS study which showed that "[r]espondents from a higher socio-economic status were also more likely to indicate that leisure time is 'very important' in their lives relative to their less well-off peers" (Elangovan, 2021).

Impact of LOV on wellbeing

To assess the impact of LOV on Singaporeans' wellbeing, we conducted a series of regression analyses, using the nine LOV items as independent variables. The wellbeing outcomes selected as dependent variables in the regression analyses are: happiness ("All things considered, would you say that you are happy these days?" with a five-point scale of "1 = Very unhappy" to "5 = Very happy"); enjoyment ("How often do you feel you are really enjoying life these days?" on a four-point response scale of "1 = Never" to "4 = Often"); achievement ("How much do you feel you are accomplishing what you want out of life?" on a four-point scale of "1 = None" to "4 = A great deal"); level of control ("How much control do you feel you have over important aspects of your life?" on a four-point scale of "1 = None" to "4 = A great deal"); and sense of purpose ("All things considered, how much do you feel you have a sense of purpose in your life?" on a four-point scale of "1 = None" to "4 = A great deal"). As in the other chapters, the happiness scores are recoded into a 4-point scale by combining the "1s" and "2s" into a single category prior to data analysis. These five outcomes make up the affective aspects of wellbeing.

The cognitive aspect of wellbeing was measured with the five-item Satisfaction with Life scale (composite average of responses to five statements). The five statements in the scale are as follows: "In most ways, my life is close to my ideal", "The conditions of my life are excellent", "I am satisfied with my life", "So far I have gotten the important things I want in life" and "If I could live my life over, I would change almost nothing". Each item was rated on a six-point scale "1 = Strongly disagree" to "6 = Strongly agree").

LOV and affective wellbeing

As shown in Table 5.4, there was remarkable consistency in the effects of the nine values on each of the affective aspects of wellbeing. The values of sense of belonging and excitement were consistently significant predictors. Singaporeans who valued a sense of belonging and excitement tended to be happier, enjoyed life more, had a greater sense of achievement and perceived greater control and purpose in their lives. Apart from the level of enjoyment, valuing a sense of accomplishment also positively predicted Singaporeans' happiness, achievement, control and purpose in life. Singaporeans who sought warm relationships with others also tended to be happier, while those that strived for self-fulfillment tended to have greater levels of enjoyment. The values of security, self-respect, fun and enjoyment, and being well-respected did not significantly impact any affective aspects of wellbeing.

LOV and cognitive wellbeing

We observed similar patterns of results for the regressions involving cognitive wellbeing (Table 5.4). The values of sense of belonging and excitement positively influenced respondents' scores for satisfaction with life. Being well-respected was the only other value that was significantly associated with satisfaction with life; those that valued being well-respected tended to be more satisfied with their lives.

Conclusion

We have investigated Singaporeans' ranking of the importance of the LOV items over the past three QOL Surveys (2011, 2016 and 2022). Several issues are worth highlighting when we examined these past rankings. While Singaporeans' rankings of the top two values of security and self-respect have not changed over the past decade, they have also consistently given lowest priority to the two values of fun and enjoyment and excitement. The low focus on leisure also seems to be common among Asian countries like China and Japan, as well as ASEAN countries like Malaysia and Thailand.

In 2022, age, gender, education and marital status had differential impact on the nine values in the LOV (self-respect, security, being well-respected, warm relationships with others, sense of accomplishment, self-fulfillment, sense of belonging, fun and enjoyment, and excitement). A deep dive into the 2022 QOL

Table 5.4 Impact of LOV on affective and cognitive wellbeing (2022)

LOV items	Unstandardized Beta					
	Happiness	*Enjoyment*	*Achievement*	*Control*	*Purpose*	*SWL*
(Constant)	0.909	1.687	1.633	1.704	1.504	2.224
Sense of Belonging	**0.059**	**0.105**	**0.096**	**0.081**	**0.075**	**0.116**
Security	-0.011	-0.003	-0.008	-0.025	0.024	-0.052
Self-respect	-0.005	0.013	0.025	0.032	0.036	0.019
Warm Relationships with Others	**0.056**	-0.006	-0.010	-0.002	0.005	-0.027
Fun and Enjoyment	0.010	0.017	-0.003	-0.010	-0.013	0.012
Being Well-respected	0.006	-0.005	0.009	0.009	0.029	**0.067**
Sense of Accomplishment	**0.100**	0.034	**0.075**	**0.053**	**0.083**	0.045
Self-fulfilment	0.026	**0.063**	0.009	0.037	0.011	0.014
Excitement	**0.084**	**0.044**	**0.057**	**0.082**	**0.055**	**0.204**
R^2	0.083***	0.076***	0.075***	0.079***	0.095***	0.116***

Note: Bold figures indicate statistical significance. SWL = Satisfaction with Life Scale.
*** $p < 0.001$.

survey data revealed that Singaporeans who were male, younger, better educated and had higher household incomes tended to place more importance on fun and enjoyment and excitement than other Singaporeans. Hence, it seems to imply that apart from gender, resourcefulness, which was facilitated by better education and higher income, do influence Singaporeans to place more emphasis on fun and enjoyment and excitement. Perhaps better education and higher income have been achieved at the expense of having more leisure time, potentially explaining the heightened appreciation of fun and enjoyment and excitement among the more financially well-endowed Singaporeans.

In 2022, different values of LOV have differential effects on Singaporeans' wellbeing. Sense of belonging and, surprisingly, excitement were the two values that consistently had a significant influence on Singaporeans' satisfaction with life, happiness, enjoyment, achievement, control and purpose, while sense of accomplishment consistently had a positive impact on Singaporeans' achievement, control and purpose. Warm relationships with others had a significant and positive impact only on Singaporeans' happiness. Being well-respected only influenced Singaporean's cognitive wellbeing (i.e., satisfaction with life) but not affective wellbeing. Surprisingly, the value of security, which was ranked number one in 2022, and self-respect, which was ranked number two in 2022, had no significant impact on Singaporeans' wellbeing.

References

Cleaver, M., & Muller, T.E. (2002). "I want to pretend I'm eleven years younger: subjective age and seniors' motives for vacation travel". *Social Indicators Research, 60,* 227–241.

Elangovan, N. (2021, 3 February). "Family still top priority for Singaporeans, but importance of work has declined since 2002: IPS Study". TODAY. Retrieved 1 May 2023, from www.todayonline.com/singapore/family-still-top-priority-singaporeans-importance-work-has-declined-2002-ips-survey

Gurel-Atay, E., Xie, G. X., Chen, J., & Kahle, L. R. (2010). "Changes in social values in the United States, 1976–2007". *Journal of Advertising Research, 50*(1), 57–67.

Haerpfer, C., Inglehart, R., Moreno, A., Welzel, C., Kizilova, K., Diez-Medrano J., Lagos, M., Norris, P., Ponarin, P., & Puranen, B. (Eds.). (2022). *World Values Survey: Round seven–country-pooled datafile version 5.0.* Madrid, Spain & Vienna, Austria: JD Systems Institute & WVSA Secretariat.

Kahle, L. R. (1983). *Social values and social change: adaptation to life in America.* New York: Praeger.

Kahle, L. R. (1996). "Social values and consumer behavior: Research from the list of values". In: C. Seligman, J.M. Olson, & M.P Zanna (Eds.), *The psychology of values: The Ontario Symposium, 8* (pp. 135–151) Mahwah, NJ: Lawrence Erlbaum Associates.

Mitchell, A. (1983). *The nine American lifestyles.* New York: Macmillan.

Rokeach, M. (1968). *Beliefs, attitudes, values.* San Francisco: Jossey-Bass.

Rokeach, M. (1973). *The nature of human values.* New York: Free Press.

Schwartz, S.H. (2007). "Value orientations: measurement, antecedents and consequences across nations". In R. Jowell, C. Roberts, R. Fitzgerald, & G. Eva (Eds.), *Measuring attitudes cross-nationally–lessons from the European Social Survey* (pp. 169–203). London: Sage.

Stockard, J., Carpenter, C., & Kahle, L. (2014). "Continuity and change in values in midlife: Testing the age stability hypothesis". *Experimental Aging Research, 40*(2), 224–244.

Sudbury, L., & Simcock, P. (2009). "Understanding older consumers through cognitive age and the list of values: A U.K.-based Perspective". *Psychology and Marketing, 20*(1), 22–38.

6   Clustering of Singaporeans

In this chapter, we continue our inquiry into the influence of values on wellbeing. While Chapter 5 included nine values that signify personal strivings, we examine value orientations on a broader scale by measuring Singaporeans' inclination toward four major aspects of life (i.e., family, sustainability, tradition and material consumption) and using them to distinguish among clusters of Singaporeans. Various value orientations had been used for the clustering of Singaporeans in the past two QOL Surveys (2011 and 2016). Some value orientations are more pro-social and other-oriented, while some are more self-centered. For the 2022 QOL Survey, respondents were asked for their views on 28 statements on various value orientations. These include family values, concern about the environment (or eco-orientation), materialism, societal consciousness and traditionalism. All statements used to measure value orientations in the 2016 QOL Survey were retained, except for the three statements on entrepreneurial spirit ("I am creative and resourceful in solving problems", "I have more self-confidence than most people" and "To me, realizing my fullest potential is more important than monetary rewards"). These statements were dropped based on a review of the relevance and saliency of the value orientation observed in the past surveys. The responses ranged from "1" for "Strongly Disagree" to "6" for "Strongly Agree". Higher means thus indicated greater agreement about a particular statement.

Identification of factors

Exploratory factor analysis (EFA) with principal axis factoring extraction was conducted to derive the respective underlying

DOI: 10.4324/9781003399650-6

dimensions of Singaporeans' value orientations. The EFA of the 28 statements yielded four factors with eigenvalues above one, and the four factors explained 60.81 per cent of the variance of the 28 statements. All statements had a factor loading of at least 0.4 and did not cross load on multiple factors. The four factors, the statements measuring the value orientations, their loadings and reliability alphas are indicated in Table 6.1. These factors and value orientations were then used to organize Singaporeans into the distinctive clusters.

- Family Values (Factor 1): This factor has seven statements similar to the family values factor derived in the 2011 and 2016 QOL Surveys.
- Sustainability (Factor 2): This factor consists of nine statements that measured sustainability-related values, like environmental sustainability and social sustainability. The sustainability factor in this survey subsumes the eco-orientation and volunteerism factors found in the 2016 QOL Survey into a single factor.
- Traditionalism (Factor 3): This factor has all the five statements that made up the traditionalism factor in the 2016 QOL Survey.
- Materialism (Factor 4): This factor contains seven statements and combines the status consciousness factor in the 2016 QOL Survey with the materialism factor.

As described earlier, two of the four factors (i.e., family values and traditionalism) in the 2022 QOL Survey are identical to their 2016 counterparts and are measured by the same statements on value orientations. The remaining two factors (i.e., sustainability and materialism) are formed through combining smaller factors in 2016 into larger factors in the present survey.

Generally, there was some stability in the value orientations being measured, as the statements within each value orientation remained about the same over the years. Factor analyses showed that it is psychometrically sound to apply the four-factor structure (i.e., family values, sustainability, traditionalism and materialism) to the same 28 statements in the 2011 and 2016 QOL Surveys. Hence, in the sections to follow, we describe each factor in detail and how they compare with the 2011 and 2016 QOL Surveys based on the four-factor structure.

Table 6.1 Four-factor structure of value orientations (2022) and mean scores (2011, 2016, 2022)

Factors and Value Orientations	2022 Factor loadings	2022 Mean score (rank)	2016 Mean score (rank)	2011 Mean score (rank)
Factor 1: Family Values (Cronbach's α = 0.91)		5.00	5.34	5.15
Family members should stand by one another through the ups and downs in life.	0.839	5.09 (1)	5.40 (2)	5.23 (2)
Family love makes a person feel appreciated and treasured.	0.805	5.08 (2)	5.39 (4)	5.20 (4)
One should support one's parents in their old age.	0.756	5.08 (2)	5.40 (2)	5.28 (1)
One should honor one's parents and grandparents.	0.768	5.05 (4)	5.43 (1)	5.23 (2)
Family members should communicate openly and honestly with each other.	0.760	5.02 (5)	5.27 (6)	5.09 (5)
One should strive to provide the best for one's children.	0.680	4.89 (6)	5.32 (5)	4.97 (7)
Family members should be prepared to make sacrifices to help each other.	0.676	4.80 (7)	5.19 (7)	5.02 (6)

Factor 2: Sustainability (Cronbach's α = 0.90)		4.06	4.09	4.09
I would be willing to bring my own bags for shopping to reduce the use of non-recyclable bags.	0.758	4.58 (1)	4.24 (2)	4.25 (3)
I will stop buying my favorite brand if I know the company producing it was polluting the environment.	0.707	4.30 (2)	4.43 (1)	4.34 (1)
I feel I should do my part to help raise funds for charity.	0.630	4.08 (3)	4.16 (5)	4.30 (2)
I usually buy products that use recyclable packaging.	0.796	4.02 (4)	4.08 (7)	3.95 (8)
I would be willing to use a non-polluting detergent even if I have my laundry less white.	0.689	4.02 (4)	4.10 (6)	4.00 (6)
I am willing to do volunteer work on a regular basis.	0.719	3.98 (6)	3.89 (8)	3.96 (7)
I am willing to pay more for products that are friendly to the environment.	0.782	3.96 (7)	4.17 (3)	4.15 (4)
I often donate money for charitable causes.	0.540	3.96 (7)	4.17 (3)	4.12 (5)
I often find time to be involved in community or charity work.	0.604	3.66 (9)	3.61 (9)	3.77 (9)

(*Continued*)

Table 6.1 (Continued)

Factors and Value Orientations	2022 Factor loadings	2022 Mean score (rank)	2016 Mean score (rank)	2011 Mean score (rank)
Factor 3: Traditionalism (Cronbach's α = 0.80)		3.98	4.22	4.08
I celebrate festivals in the traditional way.	0.483	4.27 (1)	4.46 (1)	4.36 (1)
Religion is an important part of my life.	0.699	4.24 (2)	4.42 (2)	4.21 (2)
I like to stick to traditional ways of doing things.	0.480	4.09 (3)	4.13 (4)	3.94 (4)
It is wrong to have sex before marriage.	0.796	3.85 (4)	4.21 (3)	4.13 (3)
Divorce is unacceptable.	0.742	3.46 (5)	3.90 (5)	3.77 (5)
Factor 4: Materialism (Cronbach's α = 0.88)		3.61	3.27	3.56
Money can solve most people's problems.	0.601	4.30 (1)	4.04 (1)	4.32 (1)
If I had to choose between having more money and leisure, I would choose more money.	0.587	4.02 (2)	3.71 (2)	3.94 (2)

Statement				
My social status is an important part of my life.	0.707	3.58 (3)	3.62 (3)	3.94 (2)
I admire people who own expensive homes, cars and clothes.	0.771	3.46 (4)	2.92 (5)	3.20 (5)
I feel good if the credit card I use gives the impression of high status with exclusive privileges.	0.764	3.39 (5)	2.57 (7)	3.03 (7)
I like to own things that impress people.	0.817	3.30 (6)	2.88 (6)	3.33 (4)
I usually look out for well-known brands to reflect my status in life.	0.744	3.22 (7)	3.15 (4)	3.17 (6)

Note: Ranks were sorted in descending order of the means of statements in each factor in 2022. Each statement was rated on a 6-point Likert scale (1 = Strongly Disagree, 6 = Strongly Agree).

Family values

We start with the first factor and value orientation labeled as "family values", which is perceived to be the most important among Singaporeans (i.e., the highest mean score among the four factors in 2022). The seven statements in this value orientation were based on the Singapore government's Family Values Campaign, which was started in 1994 to enhance the wellbeing of families and underpin the progress of Singapore. We have used the same statements for the family values orientation for the 2011 and 2016 QOL Surveys. As shown in Table 6.1, the scores for all the seven statements measuring family values and the composite score have dropped substantially in 2022 compared to 2011 and 2016. This is particularly discouraging, as the importance of family values was on a rise from 2011 to 2016, but by 2022, the gains had been reversed, and Singaporeans valued their family even less than in 2011. Despite the overall decline in family values, the statements related to standing by one's family through ups and downs, as well as providing for one's parents, were rated to be one of the most important by Singaporeans in 2022, similar to respondents in the 2011 and 2016 QOL Surveys. This emphasis on the family is also supported by the findings from a WVS conducted by the IPS from 2019 to 2020, which found that family still topped the ranking of importance (92 per cent) among the Singaporeans and Permanent Residents surveyed (Elangovan, 2021a). Singapore is not alone in reporting such a high priority placed on family. The WVS Wave 7 (2017–2022) revealed that Asian countries such as China (86.2 per cent), Japan (92 per cent) and South Korea (88.9 per cent), as well as ASEAN countries such as Indonesia (98 per cent), Malaysia (96.3 per cent) and Thailand (90.5 per cent) also shared such a family-oriented focus (Haerpfer et al., 2022).

Sustainability

The second factor and value orientation, labeled as "sustainability", comprises nine statements and is the largest out of the four value orientations in the 2022 QOL Survey (Table 6.1). This factor subsumes the factors of eco-orientation and volunteerism

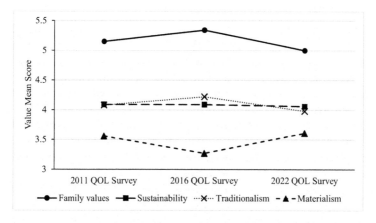

Figure 6.1 Mean scores of value orientations (2011, 2016 and 2022).

in the 2016 QOL Survey into a single construct centering around sustainability-related issues like social sustainability and environmental sustainability. Social sustainability refers to prosocial behaviors that maintain the equality and cohesiveness of our society (Grum & Babnik, 2022), whereas environmental sustainability relates to behaviors that protect and conserve our ecosystems. As seen in Figure 6.1, sustainability is the only value orientation that has remained fairly constant across 11 years and three QOL Surveys. Signifying some level of success in Singapore's campaign for the reduced use of disposable bags (National Environment Agency, 2022), in 2022, Singaporeans expressed a higher willingness to bring their own bags than in 2011 and in 2016. However, Singaporeans in 2022 were significantly less willing to incur monetary costs for sustainability-related purposes, such as donating money for charitable causes and paying more for environmentally friendly products. Coincidentally, according to the WVS 2017–2022, the low willingness to donate money is also prevalent across some Asian countries like Japan (45.3 per cent said they have donated to a group or campaign) and South Korea (16.1 per cent) and ASEAN countries like Indonesia (14.8 per cent), Thailand (28 per cent) and Malaysia (42.7 per cent, Haerpfer et al., 2022).

Traditionalism

The third factor and value orientation that emerged is labeled "traditionalism". This value orientation consists of the exact five statements in the 2016 QOL Survey, and measures views about divorce, premarital sex, traditions, and religion. The composite Traditionalism score as well as each of the statements under this factor seem to follow an inverted U-shaped pattern, whereby Singaporeans became more traditional from 2011 to 2016, and then decreased in their traditionalism from 2016 to 2022. Notably, respondents in the 2022 QOL Survey have become more liberal in their stance towards divorce and pre-marital sex than respondents in 2011 and 2016. Interestingly, the same WVS mentioned earlier found that "Singaporeans remain largely conservative on issues such as homosexuality, abortion, casual sex and prostitution, but deem the likes of divorce, euthanasia and the death penalty as more acceptable" (Ong, 2021). In contrast, according to the WVS 2017–2022, while an Asian country like Japan is more liberal on issues like divorce (23.8 per cent deemed it a justifiable cause), other Asian countries are less liberal on such issues. A third of those surveyed in China deemed divorce as "never justifiable" and close to a third (27.7 per cent) in South Korea deemed it less justifiable. Among ASEAN countries, Indonesia is the least tolerant of divorce, where close to half (49.1 per cent) deemed divorce to be "never justifiable", while only 16.8 per cent in Malaysia, 27.9 per cent in Singapore and 24.7 per cent in Thailand shared such sentiments (Haerpfer et al., 2022). As far as casual sex is concerned, the WVS 2017–2022 revealed that among Asian countries such as China, Japan and South Korea, the Chinese were the least liberal on this issue, with more than a third (40.3 per cent) claiming that such an act is "never justifiable", while those sharing such sentiments in Japan and South Korea were among the minority (5.2 per cent for Japan and 5.1 percent for South Korea). Among ASEAN countries, Indonesians were the least liberal, with more than three-quarters (76.5 per cent) claiming that such acts are "never justifiable", while only 31.8 per cent in Malaysia, 34 per cent in Singapore and 26.2 per cent in Thailand shared such sentiments (Haerpfer et al., 2022).

Despite the overall drop in traditionalism in 2022, the relative rankings of the five statements remained relatively constant over the years, with Singaporeans placing greatest importance on (1) celebrating festivals in traditional ways and (2) in religion out of the five statements. Among some ASEAN countries surveyed in the WVS 2017–2022, Indonesia and Malaysia, both countries with a large majority of Muslims, reported religion as "very important" (98.1 per cent for Indonesia and 72.4 per cent for Malaysia), whereas among some Asian countries, religion is rated "not important at all" in China (42.8 per cent) and Japan (42.1 per cent), and "not very important" in South Korea (47.7 per cent, Haerpfer et al., 2022).

Materialism

The fourth and final factor and value orientation in the 2022 QOL Survey is "materialism". This value orientation is made up of a total of seven statements that measured the factors of status consciousness and materialism in the 2016 QOL Survey. As seen in Figure 6.1, while all other values either remained constant or decreased in importance, materialism is the only value orientation that Singaporeans placed greater emphasis on in 2022 than in the past years, especially more so than in 2016. Particularly, as compared to those in 2011 and 2016, respondents in the 2022 QOL Survey are more likely to admire people with expensive possessions. Looking at the rankings, across the three QOL Surveys, Singaporeans constantly rated money and social status to be one of the most important among the seven statements in the materialism factor. This materialistic orientation is not surprising given that besides family and friends, Singaporeans ranked wealth as their top three priorities in the previously mentioned WVS (Elangovan, 2021a).

Identification of clusters

With the confirmation of the four value orientations, a two-step cluster analysis was conducted to identify groups of Singaporeans in the 2022 QOL Survey based on the respective composite scores of family values, sustainability, traditionalism, and materialism. Prior to the cluster analysis, ipsatization of the responses to the 28 value orientations was conducted to account for any response biases by the respondents. Ipsatization was conducted by subtracting each respondent's average score across the 28 statements from the raw score of each value orientation statement, and the resulting scores reflect the relative importance of each of the four value orientations to an individual. Values with scores close to zero indicate average importance, while scores higher than zero reflect value orientations that are of great importance. Negative scores indicate less important values to an individual. The ipsatized mean scores of the four factors were used for cluster analysis.

Our analyses showed that a four-cluster solution provided good interpretability and also comparability with the 2011 six-cluster solution and the 2016 five-cluster solution. Each cluster was also sufficiently large. Cluster 4 was the largest group, with 622 out of 1,811 respondents (34.3 per cent) belonging to this group. This was followed by Cluster 1, with 545 respondents (30.1 per cent), and Cluster 3, with 335 respondents (18.5 per cent). Cluster 2 was the smallest group, with 309 respondents belonging to this segment (17.1 per cent). Figure 6.2 illustrates the extent to which the four value orientations are manifested in each of these clusters. An ANOVA shows that the four clusters differed on the four value

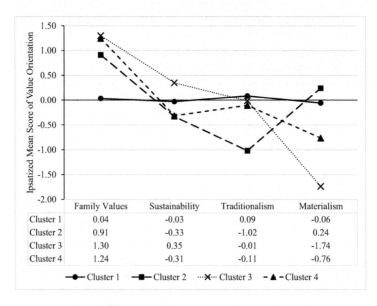

	Family Values	Sustainability	Traditionalism	Materialism
Cluster 1	0.04	-0.03	0.09	-0.06
Cluster 2	0.91	-0.33	-1.02	0.24
Cluster 3	1.30	0.35	-0.01	-1.74
Cluster 4	1.24	-0.31	-0.11	-0.76

Figure 6.2 Clusters of Singaporeans (2022).

orientations to varying extents, which we will elaborate on in the following section.

Description of clusters

Cluster 1: The Balancers

This group of Singaporeans (30.1 per cent) perceived the four value orientations to be similarly important in their lives. Alongside Cluster 3, they were the most traditional among the four clusters. Singaporeans in Cluster 1 also ranked 2nd highest in sustainability and materialism, and were the least family-oriented. Their scores were relatively stable across the four value orientations, with no strong distinctive characteristics, earning them the label "the Balancers".

Demographically as shown in Table 6.2, males were significantly more likely to be classified to this segment. Compared to the overall age distribution of the weighted sample (which has been adjusted towards the national statistics), a greater proportion of the Balancers was aged between 21 and 39 years old, suggesting that this cluster comprised younger adults. The Distribution of marital status fairly resembled the overall sample's distribution as almost two-thirds of this group were married. Adults in this cluster were also more highly educated and had higher household income than the other clusters.

Cluster 2: The Materialists

Singaporeans in Cluster 2 ranked the highest on materialism while they ranked the second lowest on family values and the lowest on sustainability and traditionalism. Thus, this cluster was named "the Materialists". The Materialists made up the smallest cluster in the 2022 QOL Survey, with 17.1 per cent of the respondents belonging to this group.

Several demographic attributes differentiate this cluster from the rest. While males and females were equally likely to be a Materialist, Singaporeans in this group were more likely to be single and highly educated, as compared to the other clusters. Similar to Cluster 1, the Balancers, members of Cluster 2 were also younger than Singaporeans in Clusters 3 and 4. Only 9.4 per

Table 6.2 Demographic profiles of clusters (2022)

Demographics	Cluster 1 (n = 545)	Cluster 2 (n = 309)	Cluster 3 (n = 335)	Cluster 4 (n = 622)	Total (n = 1811)
Gender					
- Male	301 (55.2%)	157 (50.8%)	147 (44.0%)	273 (43.8%)	878 (48.5%)
- Female	244 (44.8%)	152 (49.2%)	187 (56.0%)	350 (56.2%)	933 (51.5%)
Marital Status					
- Single	200 (34.7%)	147 (47.6%)	110 (32.9%)	233 (37.5%)	690 (38.1%)
- Married	345 (63.3%)	162 (52.4%)	224 (67.1%)	389 (62.5%)	1120 (61.9%)
Age Group					
- 21 to 29	129 (23.7%)	94 (30.4%)	34 (10.1%)	62 (10.0%)	319 (17.6%)
- 30 to 39	158 (29.0%)	78 (25.2%)	37 (11.0%)	92 (14.8%)	365 (20.2%)
- 40 to 49	124 (22.8%)	72 (23.3%)	55 (16.4%)	116 (18.6%)	367 (20.3%)
- 50 to 59	75 (13.8%)	28 (9.1%)	92 (27.5%)	167 (26.8%)	362 (20.0%)
- 60 to 69	43 (7.9%)	30 (9.7%)	97 (29.0%)	152 (24.4%)	322 (17.8%)
- 70 to 79	15 (2.8%)	7 (2.3%)	20 (6.0%)	33 (5.3%)	75 (4.1%)

Education					
- Low	99 (18.2%)	44 (14.2%)	75 (22.4%)	143 (23.0%)	361 (19.9%)
- Medium	104 (19.1%)	58 (18.8%)	97 (29.0%)	166 (26.7%)	425 (23.5%)
- High	342 (62.8%)	207 (67.0%)	163 (48.7%)	313 (50.03%)	1025 (56.6%)
Household Income					
- Low	75 (13.8%)	29 (9.4%)	51 (15.3%)	98 (15.8%)	253 (14.0%)
- Low-Medium	158 (29.0%)	99 (32.1%)	134 (40.1%)	222 (35.7%)	613 (33.9%)
- Medium-High	218 (40.1%)	128 (41.6%)	91 (27.2%)	228 (36.7%)	665 (36.8%)
- High	93 (17.1%)	52 (16.9%)	58 (17.4%)	74 (11.9%)	277 (15.3%)

cent of the Materialists had a low household income as compared to other clusters (13.8 per cent to 15.8 per cent), suggesting that Singaporean adults in this cluster tended to enjoy better socio-economic status.

Cluster 3: The Pro-Social Family-Oriented

Cluster 3 was one of the two clusters that scored extremely highly on family values. Ranked the first on family values, Cluster 3, which represented 18.5 per cent of respondents in the 2022 QOL Survey, also had the highest score on sustainability, indicating a strong focus on family and also an outward-looking perspective in terms of caring for others and the environment. They had average scores on traditionalism and the lowest on materialism. With a focus on family, others and the environment, as well as an anticonsumption orientation, this cluster was labeled "the Pro-Social Family-Oriented".

Members of Cluster 3 tended to be female, older, less educated and of lower household income. More than half of the respondents in Cluster 3 were females, aged 50 and above, and had a household income that is categorized to be low or low-medium. Less than half of Cluster 3 (48.7 per cent) have received a university education, significantly less than the proportions of degree holders in Clusters 1 and 2. The distribution of marital status in Cluster 3 fairly resembled the overall sample's distribution, with 67.1 per cent of Singaporeans in this cluster being married.

Cluster 4: The Traditional Family-Oriented

Cluster 4 was similar to Cluster 3, as both groups were high scorers on family values and traditionalism. However, while the Pro-Social Family-Oriented also cared about others and the environment with a high Sustainability score, Singaporeans in Cluster 4 ranked the second lowest in sustainability. The smaller emphasis on sustainability by this group of adults was compensated by their increased focus on materialism as they ranked 3rd on this value orientation. Thus, Cluster 4 which made up 34.3 per cent of the sample, has been named "the Traditional Family-Oriented".

Members of Cluster 4 share many demographic similarities with those of Cluster 3. Compared to those in Clusters 1 and 2,

Singaporeans grouped in Cluster 4 were more significantly likely to be female, older and less educated. Marital status and house-hold income of this group followed the distribution of the overall sample relatively closely.

Comparison of clusters on affective and cognitive wellbeing, satisfaction with economic wellbeing and trust

Affective and cognitive wellbeing

We start by comparing the four clusters on the cognitive and affective aspects of wellbeing. Specifically, we examine if clusters of Singaporeans with varying value orientation profiles would differ in their cognitive and affective wellbeing. As in the other chapters, cognitive wellbeing was measured using the five-item Satisfaction with Life scale (1 = "Strongly Disagree", 6 = "Strongly Agree"). We also looked at another aspect of cognitive wellbeing through the Life Evaluation Index (based on the Cantril Self-Anchoring Striving Scale) mentioned in the Gallup-Healthways Well-Being Index. Respondents were asked to evaluate their present and future (five years from now) lives on a ladder with numbers 0 (worst possible life) to 10 (best possible life). Affective wellbeing was measured as participants' responses for wellbeing outcomes such as happiness, enjoyment, achievement, control and purpose. Possible scores for each of these scales ranged from one to four, with higher values indicating better wellbeing.

As seen in Figure 6.3 (solid line), the Balancers (i.e., Cluster 1) were the most satisfied with life among the four clusters, followed by the Pro-Social Family-Oriented (Cluster 3) and then the Traditional Family-Oriented (Cluster 4) and the Materialists (Cluster 2). Along with the Pro-Social Family-Oriented, the Balancers also rated their lives now on the Cantril Ladder to be significantly better than the Traditional Family-Oriented and the Materialists (Figure 6.3, white bar). As an indication that Singaporeans were generally hopeful of their future, all four clusters perceived their lives five years from now to be significantly better than their lives now (Figure 6.3, gray bar). Notably, this sense of hopefulness was more pronounced among the Materialists and the Traditional Family-Oriented, as these two groups of Singaporeans expected their lives to improve the most in five years' time.

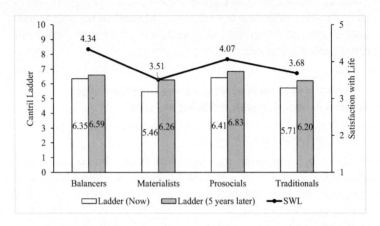

Figure 6.3 Comparison of clusters across cognitive aspects of wellbeing (2022).Note: SWL = Satisfaction with Life Scale. SWL scores ranged from 1 to 5. Ladder scores ranged from 0 (worst) to 10 (best).

On the affective aspects (Figure 6.4), however, the Pro-Social Family-Oriented consistently stood out as the segment with the best wellbeing. Singaporeans in this cluster significantly enjoyed life more, felt more accomplished in life, had more control over their lives and had greater purpose in life than the Traditional Family-Oriented and the Materialist groups. Although the Balancers were as happy as the Pro-Social Family-Oriented, the Balancers did not perform as well as the Pro-Social Family-Oriented in the other aspects of affective wellbeing. Given that Singaporeans who valued sustainability the most (Pro-Social Family Oriented) had the best affective wellbeing, this suggests that engaging in pro-social behaviors may be one way that Singaporeans can leverage on to improve their happiness.

Finally, the Materialists consistently ranked the last across all indices of wellbeing (Figure 6.4). Respondents who placed great importance on improving their social status through material possessions tended to be less satisfied with life, more unhappy, enjoyed life less, perceived that they accomplished less, felt less in control and had less purpose in life than other Singaporeans. However, given the nature of the QOL Survey, we should be careful about making any causal claims of materialism on happiness. On

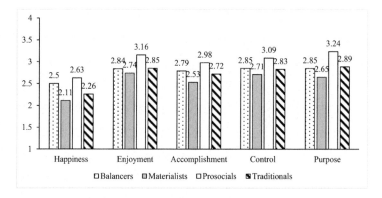

Figure 6.4 Comparison of clusters across affective aspects of wellbeing (2022).

the one hand, Materialists might be more unhappy than others because they were unable to satisfy their incessant pursuit for branded and more expensive items. On the other hand, it was also possible that respondents in the Materialists cluster might have been unhappy to begin with and they turned to material possessions as a means to improve their wellbeing. Either way, the findings suggest that owning more material possessions may not be a good way to make one happier.

Satisfaction with economic wellbeing

To measure economic wellbeing, we asked respondents four questions: (1) "Do you/your household have enough money to buy the things you need?"; (2) "If you/your household have/has a loan, are you/your household currently able to meet these monthly/regular financial commitments as planned?"; (3) "Do you/your household have more than enough money to do what you want to do?" and (4) "Would you/your household be able right now to make a major purchase, such as a car, appliance or furniture, or pay for a significant home repair if you needed to?" Answering "Yes" to these questions would reflect satisfaction with economic wellbeing.

Singaporeans in the four clusters differed drastically in satisfaction with their economic wellbeing. As seen in Figure 6.5, the

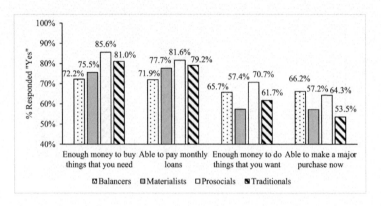

Figure 6.5 Satisfaction with economic wellbeing across clusters (2022).

Pro-Social Family-Oriented tend to be the most satisfied with their economic wellbeing, as this segment of Singaporeans had the greatest proportion indicating that they had enough to buy what they need, to pay loans, to do things that they want and to make big purchases now. In the Pro-Social Family-Oriented cluster, 85.6 per cent indicated that they had enough money to buy things that they need, significantly more than 72.2 per cent of the Balancers and 75.5 per cent of the Materialists. Notably, these two clusters (i.e., Balancers and Materialists) had higher household income than the Pro-Social Family-Oriented (Table 6.2). Yet they were less satisfied with their economic wellbeing. With the Materialists consistently being among the two least satisfied clusters across the four economic wellbeing indicators, this potentially explains the poor cognitive and affective wellbeing of Singaporeans in this cluster.

Generalized trust

Finally, we compared the extent to which each cluster trusts others in general. As far as trusting other individuals is concerned (Figure 6.6), respondents of the 2022 QOL Survey tended to be skeptical of others, with more than half of almost every cluster disagreeing that people can be trusted, people would be fair and that people would try to be helpful. More than half of the Pro-Social

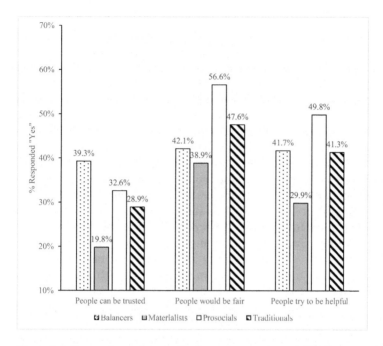

Figure 6.6 Comparison of generalized trust across clusters (2022).

Family-Oriented thought that most people would be fair (56.6 per cent), significantly more than the proportions of the Balancers and the Materialists who thought so. This low trust in others was also found by IPS's WVS of more than 2,000 Singaporeans from November 2019 to March 2020: "[t]here is an overall low level of trust among Singaporeans for others, with two-thirds (64.9 per cent) of respondents to a study saying that they felt they had to be very careful when dealing with people, as opposed to feeling most people could be trusted" (Elangovan, 2021b). Interestingly, except for China, where close to two-thirds (63.5 per cent) said that most people can be trusted, most of the other Asian countries (Japan 61.0 per cent) and South Korea (67.1 per cent), and ASEAN countries (Indonesia (95.3 per cent), Malaysia (80.4 per cent) and Thailand (65.6 per cent) shared that they needed to be very careful when dealing with people (Haerpfer et al., 2022).

Conclusion

In this chapter, we reported the value orientations and clustering of Singaporeans in 2022. Factor analysis showed four value orientations based on the 2022 QOL Survey data: (1) family values; (2) sustainability; (3) traditionalism and (4) materialism. Four different segments of Singaporeans emerged based on a clustering analysis of the four value orientations. Out of these four value orientations, two of them, namely, family values and traditionalism, are identical to their counterparts in 2016 and are measured by the same value orientation statements. In fact, the 2001 QOL Survey on Singaporeans also found these two value orientations to be part of the important factors in the clustering of Singaporeans (Tambyah & Tan, 2018). This shows the persistence of these two value orientations among Singaporeans across the decades.

Another factor worthy of mention is the sustainability value orientation, which subsumes the value orientations of eco-orientation and volunteerism in the 2011 and 2016 QOL Surveys into a single construct. The sustainability value orientation centers around sustainability-related issues like social sustainability and environmental sustainability. Regardless of whether sustainability is a single factor or a combination of eco-orientation and volunteerism factors, the scores for the items comprising the sustainability factor have remained consistently high across the decades (2011, 2016 and 2022). This signifies how Singaporeans are in tune with the increasing global concern about prosocial behaviors.

In the 2001 QOL Survey, there were eight clusters of Singaporeans, featuring two pro-family groups differentiated by their prosocial behaviors (Tambyah & Tan, 2018). In the 2011 QOL Survey, there were six clusters again featuring conservative versus new age family groups differentiated by their prosocial behaviors, and in the 2016 QOL Survey, there were the Prosocial Family-Oriented group versus the Materialistic Family-Oriented group (see Tambyah and Tan, 2018). In this 2022 QOL Survey, we have the Pro-social Family-Oriented versus the Traditional Family-Oriented groups out of four clusters. Hence, one can possibly conclude that family values, traditionalism and prosocial behaviors are time-tested, consistent and distinctive factors in the clustering of Singaporeans.

The four clusters of Singaporeans differed in their cognitive and affective wellbeing. For instance, the Balancers were the most satisfied with life among the four clusters, while the Materialists were relatively less satisfied. Although all four clusters perceived their lives five years from now to be significantly better than their lives now, this sense of hopefulness was more pronounced among the Materialists and the Traditional Family-Oriented. On the affective aspects of wellbeing, the Pro-Social Family-Oriented cluster consistently stood out as the segment with the best wellbeing. Singaporeans in this cluster significantly enjoyed life more, felt more accomplished in life, had more control over their lives and had greater purpose in life than the Traditional Family-Oriented and the Materialists.

Singaporeans in the four clusters differed drastically in satisfaction with their economic wellbeing. The Pro-Social Family-Oriented members tended to be the most satisfied with their economic wellbeing in terms of having enough to buy what they need, being able to pay monthly loans, being able to do things that they want and being able to make a major purchase now. In terms of these economic wellbeing indicators, the Materialists were consistently among the least satisfied clusters. As far as trusting other individuals are concerned, Singaporeans were generally skeptical of others as we have found in the 2016 QOL Survey. Almost every cluster in 2022 disagreed that people can be trusted, that people would be fair and that people would try to be helpful.

To give a more vivid description of the four clusters of Singaporeans derived from the 2022 QOL Survey, we describe four hypothetical individuals who are intended to serve as archetypes of each of the four clusters and are representative of the unique characteristics that distinguish each group.

Jasper is a Balancer. He is happily married and is in his mid-30s. He values his family and traditions but also enjoys the benefits of a materialistic and sustainable lifestyle. He has a medium-high household income and strives for a balanced approach to life. In general, Jasper is satisfied with his life and has a positive outlook on the future.

Nathan is a single Materialist in his late 20s. He is highly educated with a medium-high income and enjoys indulging in the finer things in life. Driven to maintain his lavish lifestyle, he often feels unfulfilled and unhappy. Despite his relative financial success, Nathan perceives himself to be in a poor financial state. Additionally, he is also distrustful of others and has a lack of concern for the environment.

May and June are sisters who share a strong family value orientation. May is highly pro-social and committed to social justice and environmental sustainability. She is passionate about making the world a better place and is often involved in community and volunteer work. May is married, in her late 60s and has a moderate income. She is content with a simple lifestyle and values her relationships with her family and community. Despite her relatively low income, she is highly satisfied with her life and is trusting of others in general.

June is May's younger sister and shares her strong family value orientation. However, unlike May, June is highly traditional and conservative in her views. She is content with her life and values her relationships with her family and community but is not particularly interested in social or environmental sustainability. June is married, in her mid-50s and has a moderate-high income. She thinks she is doing fine financially, and she does not have strong feelings regarding trusting others or not.

References

Elangovan, N. (2021a, 3 February). Family still top priority for Singaporeans, but importance of work has declined since 2002: IPS study. TODAY. Retrieved 1 May 2023, from www.todayonline.com/singapore/family-still-top-priority-singaporeans-importance-work-has-declined-2002-ips-survey

Elangovan, N. (2021b, 2 July). "Two-thirds of Singaporeans wary of trusting other people: IPS report". TODAY. Retrieved 1 May 2023, from www.todayonline.com/singapore/two-thirds-singaporeans-wary-trusting-other-people-ips-report

Grum, D. K., & Babnik, K. (2022). "The psychological concept of social sustainability in the workplace from the perspective of sustainable goals: A systematic review". *Frontiers in Psychology, 13.* https://doi.org/10.3389/fpsyg.2022.942204

Haerpfer, C., Inglehart, R., Moreno, A., Welzel, C., Kizilova, K., Diez-Medrano J., Lagos, M., Norris, P., Ponarin, P., & Puranen, B. (Eds.). 2022). *World Values Survey: Round seven–country-pooled datafile version 5.0.* Madrid, Spain & Vienna, Austria: JD Systems Institute & WVSA Secretariat.

National Environment Agency. (2022). "Minimum charge for disposable carrier bags at supermarkets to be implemented to encourage more sustainable consumption". Retrieved 1 May 2023, from www.nea.gov.sg/media/news/news/index/minimum-charge-for-disposable-carrier-bags-at-supermarkets

Ong, J. (2021). "Singapore still conservative on moral, sexuality issues, but more liberal since 2002: IPS survey". *The Straits Times.*

Tambyah, S. K., & Tan, S. J. (2018). *Happiness, wellbeing and society: What matters for Singaporeans.* London: Routledge.

7 Rights, politics and the impact on wellbeing

In this chapter, we explore the association between individual-level perceptions of issues related to democratic rights and views about politics, and their impact on the wellbeing of Singaporeans. Research has suggested that citizens living in democratic societies have a better sense of wellbeing because democracy enables the creation of conditions that contribute to wellbeing, especially the opportunities for political participation. Verba and Nie (1972) defined political participation as "the means by which the interests, desires and demands of the ordinary citizens are communicated [...] all those activities by private citizens that are more or less directly aimed at influencing the selection of governmental personnel and/or decisions they make". Political participation has been assessed in terms of the inclination or the propensity to engage in certain behaviors and/or the actual behaviors themselves. These behaviors include voting, participation in government-organized public hearings or citizens' meetings, participation in an action group, participation in a protest action, march or demonstration, working for a political campaign, contributing to a political candidate, attending a meeting or rally for a political candidate and/or contacting an elected official within the past year.

More recently, there has been a growing consensus among scholars that the definition of political participation should no longer be limited to conventional forms of participation (i.e., electoral politics). Instead, Theocharis and van Deth (2018) have expanded the concept to include unconventional political acts, such as protesting, and even various forms of civic engagement that are not obviously political in nature. Against the backdrop of

DOI: 10.4324/9781003399650-7

increased internet penetration and usage, the concept of political participation has to be adapted and extended to reflect societal circumstances (Ruess et al., 2021). For instance, nonconventional activities such as online activism and advocacy should be taken into consideration. Hooghe et al. (2014) posit that political participation is a "dynamic concept, and its classical instrumental definitions are just too restrictive in the era of digital communication technologies" (p. 345). Consistently, studies have found that younger citizens relied more heavily on online than offline political participation (Vitak et al., 2011), and that youth were more predisposed to participate in diverse nonconventional activities to influence political outcomes (Sloam, 2016). These propositions are aligned with the IPS's most recent findings on the level of democratic political engagement among the youth in the 2020 General Election, which will be briefly discussed in subsequent sections of this chapter.

Studies have shown that political participation can yield certain beneficial outcomes such as increased trust, favorable subscription to democratic values and more participation in collective action (Putnam, 2000). Teorell (2006) also suggested that individuals could view political participation as a form of self-development, personal growth and fulfillment. The perceived control that citizens in democracies have over political decision making was found to be strongly correlated to mental health and job satisfaction (Stutzer & Frey, 2006). More recently, an analysis of 2,577 interview responses across 31 provinces in the People's Republic of China has demonstrated that political participation significantly improved the life satisfaction of urban residents (He et al., 2022). The improvement was more significant for females, members of the Chinese Communist Party, the highly educated and employed individuals.

Despite the benefits of political participation, the evidence of its impact on wellbeing has been inconclusive. Although Weitz-Shapiro and Winters (2011) demonstrated that there was no relationship between voting and life satisfaction, other scholars have proposed otherwise. Pirralha (2017) explored the causal relationship between political participation and wellbeing in the Netherlands and found no substantial effect of political participation on life satisfaction. However, he suggested that political efficacy could be a potential intervening variable between political participation and wellbeing. Specifically, he demonstrated that external political efficacy and internal political efficacy both played a role at different points in time. First, the perception of the openness of the political system (i.e., external political efficacy) had an impact on individual life satisfaction. Then, believing in one's capabilities to participate (i.e., internal political efficacy) continued to play a role in influencing individual life satisfaction. Internal political efficacy also had a larger significant effect on political participation.

Barker and Martin (2011), in their review of various empirical studies, noted that political participation could promote happiness through two potential pathways. Firstly, involvement in political and social movement organizations allowed citizens to build personal relationships in addition to their usual networks associated with family, work and leisure-time activities. These relationships contributed to increased happiness given that both parties would interact over mutual interests. Another possible explanation for this causal relationship is undergirded by the idea that happiness could be derived from pursuing a good and meaningful life, which included helping others. Although participation in social movements often did not result in personal gains, individuals were driven to participate because of their belief in a larger social cause, which increased their happiness level. Lastly, Shi et al. (2022) also demonstrated through their analysis of 8,475 respondents from the 2015 Chinese Social Survey that political participation was significantly, strongly and positively correlated with satisfaction. Citizens who engaged in politics were able to increase their social capital, which, in turn, improved their physical and mental wellbeing.

Some studies have shown that the reverse relationship may hold true, for example, that happy citizens were more likely to vote and engage in other forms of political participation, which, in turn, perpetuates the democratic system (Flavin & Keane, 2012; Ward, 2019). Again, the evidence has been somewhat mixed. Pirralha (2017) found no significant effect of wellbeing on political participation. Other studies have shown that satisfied citizens were less inclined to participate in protests and strikes to achieve certain policy outcomes (Bahry & Silver, 1990), as they were in a state of "contented idleness" (Vennhovern, 1988). In contrast, Flavin and Keane (2012) showed that citizens who were satisfied were more active in turning out to vote and participate in the political process, but this participation was in activities of a nonconflicting nature (i.e., conventional political participation such as voting or giving money to political causes). Hence, the link between life satisfaction and political participation may depend on the type of political activity. Similar to Pirralha (2017), Flavin and Keane (2012) suggested that the effect of life satisfaction on political participation was mediated through political efficacy (both internal and external). In a recent study, Ward (2019) has also demonstrated that happy citizens were not only more likely to participate in voting, but they were also more likely to vote for the incumbent.

As observed in Tambyah et al. (2010), Singapore had one of the lowest rates of political participation compared to other East Asian countries like Japan, South Korea and Japan. Soon (2015) also noted the low levels of offline political participation in Singapore, whether there were elections or not. For instance, less than a quarter of voters (23.5 per cent) said they attended one or more political rallies during the 2015 General Election. Similarly for online political participation in the period leading up to polling day for the 2015 General Election, voters indicated that they followed "once a week or less" a political discussion thread, a socio-political blogger or YouTuber or shared information and commentary. However, more recently, studies that examined the level of political participation in Singapore during the 2020 General Election (GE2020) discovered three new trends: (1) a surge in digital platform engagement by political parties resulting from COVID-19 restrictions; (2) an increase in conversations on social media and (3) an increase in youth engagement. Notable studies include Soon and Neo's (2021) research on the role of digital media in GE2020, through an online survey of 2,018 Singaporean citizens above the age of 21. The authors discovered that in view of the COVID-19 restrictions, political parties ramped up their digital outreach efforts on social media platforms (such as Facebook, Instagram and Twitter). This resulted in a surge of digital platform usage among Singaporeans, which contributed to high levels of online citizen engagement. Similarly, Khoo et al. (2020) discovered an overall increase in the number of social conversations on Twitter as the polling date got nearer, with conversations discussing and responding to the campaigns of different political parties. Through interviews with 20 Singaporeans, Kwan (2022) found that youth participation during GE2020 came in the form of engaging candidates and political parties, as well as directly volunteering in party work both offline and online. In the period prior to GE2020, Singaporean youth were also involved in activism through their correspondence with political leaders and direct involvement in civic and political events. Overall, GE2020 saw 95.81 per cent of eligible voters casting their ballots, marking the highest voter turnout rate in 23 years (Tan, 2020).

Research studies on Singaporeans' views about democratic rights and politics are not common in Singapore. We have addressed this by providing the findings and insights from the 2011 QOL Survey (as reported in Tambyah & Tan, 2013), the 2016 QOL Survey (as reported in Tambyah & Tan, 2018) and the 2022 QOL Survey (as reported in this chapter). We use measures related to satisfaction with democratic rights and views about politics in our analyses, and discuss the results with comparisons to relevant local studies (e.g., the surveys conducted by IPS).

In the following sections, we present the findings on how satisfied Singaporeans are with their democratic rights, and how they view various aspects of politics. We also examine the sources of individual differences for these perceptions, and the effects of these perceptions on the wellbeing of Singaporeans.

Satisfaction with democratic rights

Democratic rights include the right to vote, to participate in any kind of organization, to gather and demonstrate, to be informed about the work and functions of government, to freedom of speech and to criticize the government. Respondents were asked about their satisfaction with these rights on a scale from 1 for "very dissatisfied" to 4 for "very satisfied". Higher means indicate higher levels of satisfaction. Consistent with the 2016 and 2011 QOL Surveys, responses collected in 2022 (see Table 7.1 and Figure 7.1) demonstrated that respondents were most satisfied with the right to vote (mean of 3.23), and least satisfied with the right to criticize the government (2.58). Similarly, satisfaction towards the right to gather and demonstrate was ranked fourth (2.65) in the list containing six different rights, while satisfaction towards freedom of speech was ranked fifth (2.64). The rankings of satisfaction regarding these four democratic rights have remained unchanged since 2011. In the 2022 QOL Survey, satisfaction with the right to be informed about the work and functions of government was ranked second (2.85), as compared to its 3rd-place ranking in 2016

Table 7.1 Satisfaction with democratic rights (percentages for 2022 and means for 2011, 2016 and 2022)

Statement	Very dissatisfied 1 %	Somewhat dissatisfied 2 %	Somewhat satisfied 3 %	Very satisfied 4 %	Mean 2022 (rank)	Mean 2016 (rank)	Mean 2011 (rank)
The right to vote	2.8	7.8	52.9	36.5	3.23 (1)	3.31 (1)	3.57 (1)
The right to participate in any kind of organization	5.8	20.0	59.2	14.9	2.83 (3)	3.12 (2)	3.27 (2)
The right to gather and demonstrate	11.6	25.6	48.6	14.2	2.65 (4)	2.75 (4)	2.96 (4)
The right to be informed about the work and functions of government	6.8	18.4	57.4	17.4	2.85 (2)	2.96 (3)	3.12 (3)
Freedom of speech	11.8	26.9	47.3	14.0	2.64 (5)	2.74 (5)	2.88 (5)
The right to criticize the government	12.3	29.1	46.6	12.0	2.58 (6)	2.62 (6)	2.68 (6)

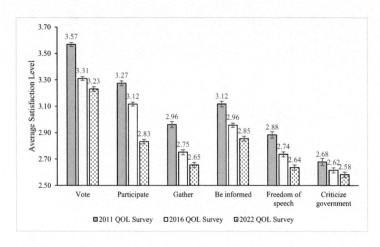

Figure 7.1 Satisfaction with democratic rights (2011, 2016 and 2022).

and 2011. Satisfaction with the right to participate in any kind of organization dropped from the 2nd placing (in 2016 and 2011) to 3rd in 2022 (2.83). In addition to the slight changes in rankings for the respondents' satisfaction with certain democratic rights, the 2022 QOL Survey has shown a decline in the level of satisfaction for all six democratic rights.

When we examined the results across demographic groups (see Tables 7.2 and 7.3), several significant differences were noted. In the 2022 QOL Survey, male and female respondents differed significantly in two aspects; females were more satisfied with the right to participate in any organization, and the right to gather and demonstrate. With regard to marital status, while those who were married tended to express higher satisfaction with all six rights, the differences between marital status were significant only for satisfaction with the right to be informed about the work and functions of government, and the right to criticize the government. In terms of age, there were no significant differences across the different age groups in relation to the satisfaction with the right to vote (see Tables 7.2 and 7.3). However, satisfaction with the other five rights followed a significant downward trend, with older respondents being less satisfied than younger respondents. On the contrary, all six rights differed significantly by education level, with the main source of difference stemming from those belonging to the highly

Table 7.2 Sources of individual differences for satisfaction with democratic rights (to vote, participate and gather) (2022)

Demographics	The right to vote	The right to participate in any kind of organization	The right to gather and demonstrate
Age			
- 20–29	3.22	2.95	2.81
- 30–39	3.27	2.99	2.81
- 40–49	3.17	2.83	2.66
- 50–59	3.23	2.79	2.55
- 60–69	3.23	2.65	2.49
- 70–79	3.35	2.62	2.41
- *F*-Stats	1.14	10.70	9.50
- *p*	0.337	< 0.001	< 0.001
Education			
- Low	3.18	2.79	2.59
- Medium	3.18	2.74	2.54
- High	3.27	2.89	2.73
- *F*-Stats	3.69	7.01	8.65
- *p*	0.025	< 0.001	< 0.001
Gender			
- Male	3.22	2.79	2.61
- Female	3.24	2.87	2.70
- *F*-Stats	0.74	4.68	4.64
- *p*	.389	.031	.031
Household Income			
- Low	3.14	2.72	2.53
- Medium-low	3.21	2.79	2.58
- Medium-high	3.26	2.86	2.71
- High	3.30	2.96	2.80
- *F*-Stats	2.82	5.26	7.36
- *p*	.038	.001	< .001
Marital Status			
- Single	3.20	2.80	2.64
- Married	3.25	2.85	2.66
- *F*-Stats	1.73	1.60	0.27
- *p*	0.189	0.206	0.605

Table 7.3 Sources of individual differences for satisfaction with democratic rights (to be informed, speak and criticize) (2022)

Demographics	The right to be informed about the work and functions of government	Freedom of speech	The right to criticize the government
Age			
- 20–29	2.95	2.78	2.71
- 30–39	2.96	2.84	2.77
- 40–49	2.79	2.60	2.58
- 50–59	2.84	2.53	2.52
- 60–69	2.74	2.49	2.37
- 70–79	2.79	2.32	2.38
- *F*-Stats	4.45	11.40	10.37
- *p*	< 0.001	< 0.001	< 0.001
Education			
- Low	2.77	2.62	2.53
- Medium	2.76	2.48	2.44
- High	2.92	2.70	2.66
- *F*-Stats	8.80	9.98	10.80
- *p*	< 0.001	< 0.001	< 0.001
Gender			
- Male	2.82	2.60	2.56
- Female	2.89	2.67	2.61
- *F*-Stats	3.30	2.35	1.61
- *p*	0.070	0.125	0.205
Household Income			
- Low	2.71	2.53	2.39
- Medium-low	2.76	2.54	2.51
- Medium-high	2.92	2.70	2.66
- High	3.03	2.78	2.74
- *F*-Stats	11.79	7.50	10.46
- *p*	< 0.001	< 0.001	< 0.001
Marital Status			
- Single	2.80	2.60	2.52
- Married	2.89	2.66	2.62
- *F*-Stats	6.04	1.76	5.17
- *p*	0.014	0.185	0.023

educated group. Compared to respondents with low or medium education levels, respondents who were more highly educated were more satisfied with all six rights in Singapore. Lastly, in relation to household income, satisfaction with each of the six rights increased in a significant linear trend from low to high household income. In other words, respondents with higher household incomes were more satisfied with their democratic rights.

The impact of democratic rights on Singaporeans' wellbeing

In this section, we examine the impact of democratic rights on Singaporeans' wellbeing by regressing the cognitive (i.e., satisfaction with life scale) and affective (i.e., happiness, enjoyment, achievement, control and purpose) aspects of wellbeing on satisfaction with each of the six rights. In general, satisfaction with democratic rights had a significant impact on Singaporeans' wellbeing, explaining at least 10 per cent of the variance (R^2 ranged from 10.7 per cent to 18 per cent) for each of the wellbeing indicators (see Table 7.4).

In terms of the impact of satisfaction with democratic rights on Singaporeans' satisfaction with life, only one of the rights did not have an impact on satisfaction with life. Whether Singaporeans were satisfied with their right to gather and demonstrate had little bearing on their satisfaction with life. However, satisfaction with all the other five democratic rights had a statistically significant and positive influence on satisfaction with life. Singaporeans' satisfaction with the right to criticize the government had the strongest influence over Singaporeans' satisfaction with life. Notably, although Singaporeans deeply cared about the right to criticize the government, they were also the least satisfied with this right among the six democratic rights measured.

By comparison, the right to vote had the greatest influence on the affective aspects of wellbeing. Consistently, satisfaction with this right had the strongest influence among the six democratic rights on Singaporeans' perceptions of happiness, enjoyment, achievement, control and purpose. Once again, satisfaction with the right to gather and demonstrate had little influence over the affective aspects of wellbeing.

Table 7.4 Regressing indicators of wellbeing on satisfaction with democratic rights (2022)

	Satisfaction with Life	Happiness	Enjoyment	Achievement	Control	Purpose
The right to vote	0.05*	0.17***	0.18***	0.14***	0.19***	0.18***
The right to participate in any kind of organization	0.06*	0.02	0.08*	0.03	0.04	0.03
The right to gather and demonstrate	0.03	-0.01	-0.06	-0.04	-0.05	-0.02
The right to be informed about the work and functions of government	0.12***	0.05	0.07*	0.12***	0.11***	0.14***
Freedom of speech	0.10**	0.14***	0.06	0.08*	0.07	0.02
The right to criticize the government	0.17***	0.10**	0.10**	0.11**	0.06	0.07*
R^2	0.180***	0.130***	0.111***	0.117***	0.107***	0.112***

Notes:
* $p < .05$. ** $p < .01$. *** $p < .001$.
Values are standardized regression coefficients.

Views about politics

In the 2022 QOL Survey, we asked Singaporeans for their views about politics on a scale of "1" (for "strongly disagree") to "5" (for "strongly agree"). These views about politics were described in seven statements that covered various aspects of politics such as the efficacy of voting, the empowerment of voters and the empathy and integrity of elected officials. Higher means indicate more agreement with the statement. We should be careful in the interpretation of the means, as we evaluate the opinions expressed in the statement about a particular aspect of politics. The percentages of agreement or disagreement can also provide additional insights. These statistics will be described and discussed in more detail in the following sections with comparisons to data from the 2011 (Tambyah & Tan, 2013) and 2016 QOL Survey (Tambyah & Tan, 2018).

The efficacy of voting

As shown in Table 7.5, Singaporeans generally take their voting duties seriously, as voting is compulsory in Singapore, and there are penalties for failing to turn up to vote. With reference to the first statement in Table 7.5 "Citizens have a duty to vote in elections", a majority of respondents for the 2022 QOL Survey have indicated "strongly agree" (34.8 per cent) or "agree" (47.8 per cent). Compared to the 2016 and 2011 QOL Surveys, there has been a decrease in the percentages of respondents who believed that citizens have a duty to vote. In the 2022 QOL Survey, there was an increase in the percentage of respondents who indicated that they "neither agree nor disagree" with the statement (13.8 per cent, as compared to 5.7 per cent in 2016 and 4.2 per cent in 2011). There was also an increase in the percentage of respondents who believed that citizens do not have a duty to vote in elections. About 2 per cent (2.2 per cent) selected "disagree", as compared to 0.2 per cent in 2016 and 0.6 per cent in 2011; 1.3 per cent selected "strongly disagree", as compared to 0.1 per cent in 2016 and 0.7 per cent in 2011). Overall, there is a decrease in the mean scores of respondents' perceptions on citizens' voting duty (4.13 in 2022, as compared to 4.22 in 2016 and 4.31 in 2011). For the second statement, "Since so many people vote in elections, it really doesn't

Table 7.5 The efficacy of voting (percentages and means) for 2011, 2016 and 2022

Statement	Strongly disagree 1 %	Disagree 2 %	Neither agree nor disagree 3 %	Agree 4 %	Strongly Agree 5 %	Mean
Citizens have a duty to vote in elections.	1.3 (0.1) [0.7]	2.2 (0.2) [0.6]	13.8 (5.7) [4.2]	47.8 (66.1) [55.7]	34.8 (27.9) [38.9]	4.13 (4.22) [4.31]
Since so many people vote in elections, it really doesn't matter whether I vote or not.	20.6 (12.9) [11.4]	28.7 (39.1) [47.3]	21.8 (19.5) [15.5]	20.9 (25.2) [19.2]	8.1 (3.3) [6.5]	2.67 (2.67) [2.62]

Note: The first set of numbers in (parentheses) are from the 2016 QOL Survey as reported in Tambyah and Tan (2018). The second set of numbers in [brackets] are from the 2011 QOL Survey as reported in Tambyah et al. (2013).

matter whether I vote or not", a majority of respondents "disagreed" (28.7 per cent) or "strongly disagreed" (20.6 per cent). The mean score (2.67) of respondents' perception on whether their votes mattered remained unchanged from the results of the 2016 QOL Survey.

With reference to the first statement "Citizens have a duty to vote in elections", age, gender and marital status did not contribute to any significant differences. However, education and household income were significant variables that affected responses towards the first statement (see Table 7.6). Specifically, respondents who were more educated were more likely to agree that they have a duty to vote. Agreement with citizens' duty to vote also increased as household income increased.

With reference to the second statement, "Since so many people vote in elections, it really doesn't matter whether I vote or not", household income and marital status did not contribute to any significant differences. Instead, age, education and gender played a statistically significant role. There was a significant negative linear correlation between age and agreement to the second statement, with younger age groups tending to agree with the statement more than the older respondents and being doubtful about whether their votes mattered. As for education, there was a significant U-shaped trend between education level and agreement to the second statement. Those with medium levels of education agreed least with the statement, which reflected their confidence in the efficacy of voting. Lastly, males were more likely to agree to this statement than females, indicating more skepticism about the efficacy of their votes.

The empowerment of the voters

In analyzing Singaporeans' sense of political empowerment, we asked respondents whether they believed that they had the power to influence policy or actions and whether they felt they could understand the local political scene (see Table 7.7). In 2022, 53.8 per cent of respondents felt less politically empowered, as demonstrated by their selection of "agree" (36 per cent) or "strongly agree" (17.8 per cent) to the statement "Generally speaking, people like me don't have the power to influence government policy or actions" (Table 7.7). Compared to results from 2011 (58 per cent) and 2016

Table 7.6 Sources of individual differences for the efficacy of voting (2022)

Demographics	Citizens have a duty to vote in elections	Since so many people vote in elections, it really doesn't matter whether I vote or not.
Age		
- 20–29	4.07	2.97
- 30–39	4.11	3.10
- 40–49	4.06	2.80
- 50–59	4.19	2.33
- 60–69	4.22	2.26
- 70–79	4.06	2.15
- *F*-Stats	2.09	30.79
- *p*	0.064	< 0.001
Education		
- Low	4.04	2.67
- Medium	4.08	2.51
- High	4.17	2.74
- *F*-Stats	4.38	5.45
- *p*	0.013	0.004
Gender		
- Male	4.11	2.75
- Female	4.14	2.60
- *F*-Stats	0.64	6.14
- *p*	0.423	0.013
Household Income		
- Low	3.94	2.69
- Medium-low	4.12	2.61
- Medium-high	4.15	2.70
- High	4.25	2.74
- *F*-Stats	6.58	0.92
- *p*	< 0.001	0.430
Marital Status		
- Single	4.09	2.66
- Married	4.15	2.68
- *F*-Stats	2.27	0.11
- *p*	0.132	0.746

Table 7.7 The empowerment of voters (percentages and means) for 2011, 2016 and 2022

Statement	Strongly disagree 1 %	Disagree 2 %	Neither agree nor disagree 3 %	Agree 4 %	Strongly Agree 5 %	Mean
Generally speaking people like me don't have the power to influence government policy or actions	4.3 (1.0) [1.9]	13.4 (11.6) [18.2]	28.5 (29.5) [21.9]	36.0 (46.7) [41.4]	17.8 (11.2) [16.6]	3.50 (3.55) [3.53]
Politics and government are so complicated that sometimes I don't understand what's happening	5.3 (1.3) [2.1]	15.3 (15.4) [25.9]	29.4 (29.1) [21.6]	38.8 (46.4) [37.3]	11.1 (7.7) [13.1]	3.35 (3.44) [3.33]

Note: The first set of numbers in (parentheses) are from the 2016 QOL Survey as reported in Tambyah and Tan (2018). The second set of numbers in [brackets] are from the 2011 QOL Survey as reported in Tambyah et al. (2013).

(57.9 per cent), there is a decrease in respondents who perceived themselves as being unable to influence political decisions. In terms of political awareness in 2022, approximately 49.9 per cent of respondents "agreed" (38.8 per cent) or "strongly agreed" (11.1 per cent) that politics was too complicated for them. However, there is a decrease in respondents who felt this way in comparison to results from 2016 (54.1 per cent) and 2011 (50.4 per cent), suggesting that Singaporeans are becoming more confident about their ability to understand the political landscape in Singapore.

In analyzing the 2021 WVS Report, Teo (2021) observed that political interest was low among Singaporeans, with politics ranking last in terms of importance in life. However, further conversations with Singaporeans revealed that they did have opinions on social issues and current affairs–they just did not perceive their opinions to be "political" in nature. Teo (2021) also discovered that the term "politics" seem to intimidate Singaporeans because they held a narrow definition of it, and were thus less confident about discussing it. This can result in a vicious cycle of dampening interest in politics, something which seems to be corroborated with the 2022 QOL Survey findings.

With reference to the statement "Generally speaking, people like me don't have the power to influence government policy or actions", significant differences were noted for age, education and household income (Table 7.8). More specifically, on the "age" variable, there was a significant linear trend with younger respondents tending to agree that they are powerless. There was also a significant negative linear trend across the differing education and household income levels. The less educated and lower-income earners felt more powerless. With reference to the statement "Politics and government are so complicated that sometimes I don't understand what's happening", significant differences were noted for age, gender and marital status. Younger respondents, females and singles tended to agree that politics was complicated compared to their respective counterparts.

The empathy and integrity of government officials

Table 7.9 shows the agreement with statements that reflect the respondents' opinions about government officials. Overall, the mean scores in 2022 for all three statements increased compared

Table 7.8 Sources of individual differences for the empowerment of voters (2022)

Demographics	Generally speaking people like me don't have the power to influence government policy or actions	Politics and government are so complicated that sometimes I don't understand what's happening
Age		
- 20–29	3.52	3.53
- 30–39	3.69	3.54
- 40–49	3.60	3.43
- 50–59	3.41	3.12
- 60–69	3.33	3.23
- 70–79	3.06	2.88
- *F*-Stats	7.77	12.92
- *p*	< 0.001	< 0.001
Education		
- Low	3.59	3.42
- Medium	3.56	3.31
- High	3.44	3.34
- *F*-Stats	3.85	1.27
- *p*	0.021	0.282
Gender		
- Male	3.49	3.30
- Female	3.50	3.40
- *F*-Stats	0.05	5.04
- *p*	0.819	0.025
Household Income		
- Low	3.68	3.43
- Medium-low	3.49	3.37
- Medium-high	3.45	3.32
- High	3.45	3.31
- *F*-Stats	3.05	0.91
- *p*	0.028	0.435
Marital Status		
- Single	3.50	3.43
- Married	3.49	3.30
- *F*-Stats	0.01	6.45
- *p*	0.913	0.011

Table 7.9 Perceived empathy and integrity of government officials (percentages and means) for 2011, 2016 and 2022

Statement	Strongly disagree 1 %	Disagree 2 %	Neither agree nor disagree 3 %	Agree 4 %	Strongly Agree 5 %	Mean
There is widespread corruption among those who govern the country	14.9 (7.7) [6.3]	23.8 (27.9) [31.9]	31.3 (46.0) [27.3]	20.5 (15.7) [27.2]	9.5 (2.7) [7.3]	2.86 (2.78) [2.97]
Generally speaking, the people who are elected to the Singapore Parliament stop thinking about the public once they're elected.	6.1 (3.4) [3.6]	17.7 (26.1) [24.7]	33.8 (37.7) [30.3]	29.3 (28.8) [30.8]	13.1 (4.0) [10.5]	3.26 (3.04) [3.20]
Government officials pay little attention to what citizens like me think.	4.3 (1.9) [2.7]	17.6 (24.6) [20.4]	30.2 (34.6) [25.8]	31.3 (33.3) [37.8]	16.6 (5.7) [13.2]	3.38 (3.16) [3.39]

Note: The first set of numbers in (parentheses) are from the 2016 QOL Survey as reported in Tambyah and Tan (2018). The second set of numbers in [brackets] are from the 2011 QOL Survey as reported in Tambyah et al. (2013).

to the 2016 scores, suggesting that Singaporeans have become more skeptical of the empathy and integrity of government officials. There was also a noticeable increase in the percentage of respondents who "strongly agreed" that there was widespread corruption among those who govern the country (9.5 per cent, compared to 2.7 per cent in 2016), that people who are elected to parliament stop thinking about the public once elected (13.1 per cent, compared to 4 per cent in 2016) and that government officials pay little attention to what citizens think (16.6 per cent, compared to 5.7 per cent in 2016). On the other end of the spectrum, there was a noticeable increase in the percentages of respondents who "strongly disagreed" with all three statements. The increase in the percentages of respondents on both ends of the spectrum suggests increasing polarization among Singaporeans in relation to their views about corruption and the empathy and integrity of government officials. Additionally, there has also been a decrease in the percentage of citizens who are "sitting on the fence" (i.e., respondents who selected "neither agree nor disagree") for all three statements, potentially suggesting an increase in political participation and opinions of Singaporeans.

Unlike in 2016, the 2022 QOL Survey responses on the perceived empathy and integrity of government officials did not differ significantly across household income and marital status. Nevertheless, significant differences were found for gender, age, and education (see Table 7.10). Males were significantly more critical of the government, perceiving the government to be more corrupted (mean score of 2.92, compared to 2.80 among females), to think less about the general public (3.31, compared to 3.20 among females), and to pay less attention to what citizens want (3.47, compared to 3.30 among females). An earlier 2010 IPS Survey also found that one out of every three Singaporeans distrusted politicians, with males being more politically cynical than females. Respondents between 30 to 39 years old agreed the most that there was widespread corruption (mean score of 3.30) and apathy among government officials (3.49 on whether government officials think about the public and 3.65 on whether government officials pay attention to citizens), with the highest mean scores across all three statements. On the contrary, respondents in the 70 to 79 years age group agreed the least, with the lowest mean scores across all three statements (2.41 for corruption, 2.71 for the empathy and integrity

Table 7.10 Sources of individual differences for perceived empathy and integrity of government officials (2022)

Demographics	There is widespread corruption among those who govern the country	Generally speaking, the people who are elected to the Singapore Parliament stop thinking about the public once they're elected.	Government officials pay little attention to what citizens like me think.
Age			
- 20–29	3.07	3.37	3.44
- 30–39	3.30	3.49	3.65
- 40–49	2.94	3.36	3.53
- 50–59	2.61	3.13	3.18
- 60–69	2.44	3.04	3.24
- 70–79	2.41	2.71	2.71
- *F*-Stats	27.98	12.65	16.14
- *p*	< 0.001	< 0.001	< 0.001
Education			
- Low	2.80	3.14	3.33
- Medium	2.85	3.24	3.43
- High	2.88	3.31	3.38
- *F*-Stats	0.63	3.28	0.71
- *p*	0.533	0.038	0.492
Gender			
- Male	2.92	3.31	3.47
- Female	2.80	3.20	3.30
- *F*-Stats	4.46	4.87	12.00
- *p*	0.035	0.021	< 0.001
Household Income			
- Low	2.84	3.20	3.40
- Medium-low	2.86	3.26	3.40
- Medium-high	2.85	3.26	3.36
- High	2.91	3.31	3.40
- *F*-Stats	0.24	0.45	0.23
- *p*	0.866	0.718	0.875
Marital Status			
- Single	2.89	3.24	3.41
- Married	2.84	3.26	3.37
- *F*-Stats	0.54	0.15	0.44
- *p*	0.461	0.702	0.506

of government officials). In general, there was a significant downward trend, with older respondents agreeing less to the statements. In terms of education, differing education levels were significant only in relation to the statement on whether government officials think about the public once elected to office. Respondents with higher education levels tended to agree more with this statement (mean score of 3.31, as compared to 3.24 for medium education levels and 3.14 for respondents with low education levels).

The impact of views about politics on Singaporeans' wellbeing

To examine how views about politics are correlated with Singaporeans' wellbeing, we conducted several regression analyses, using responses to the seven statements on views about politics as independent variables and the various wellbeing outcomes (i.e., satisfaction with life, happiness, enjoyment, achievement, control and purpose) as the dependent variables. For easier understanding, Statements 2 to 7 in the views about politics section were reverse coded for this analysis such that higher scores on all seven statements reflected more positive views about politics. Table 7.11 shows the results of the regression analyses. In general, Singaporeans' perceptions about politics had significant, albeit small, influences on their wellbeing.

The perception of having the power to influence politics in Singapore had a strong impact on Singaporeans' wellbeing. Across the six regressions, perceiving (1) citizens to have a duty to vote and (2) regular Singaporeans to have the power to influence government policy or actions were the only two associations that consistently influenced all six wellbeing outcomes. In other words, Singaporeans who feel a stronger sense of duty to vote and think that they can influence policy tend to have higher satisfaction with life, to be happier and to perceive greater enjoyment, achievement, control, and purpose in their lives.

Conclusion

There has been a dip in the "satisfaction with democratic rights" from 2011 to 2016. The slide seems to have continued in 2022. The 2022 QOL Survey results showed a decline in the level of satisfaction for all six democratic rights, with some small changes in

Table 7.11 Impact of views about politics on Singaporeans' wellbeing (2022)

	Satisfaction with Life	Happiness	Enjoyment	Achievement	Control	Purpose
Citizens have a duty to vote in elections.	0.26***	0.26***	0.25***	0.24***	0.25***	0.26***
There is widespread corruption among those who govern the country (R)	−0.12***	−0.08*	−0.02	−0.04	−0.04	−0.02
Generally speaking, people like me don't have the power to influence government policy or actions (R)	0.19***	0.14***	0.15***	0.16***	0.17***	0.13***
Politics and government are so complicated that sometimes I don't understand what's happening (R)	−0.01	0.02	0.06*	0.04	0.04	0.05
Since so many people vote in elections, it really doesn't matter whether I vote or not. (R)	−0.29***	−0.13***	−0.06*	−0.08**	−0.10**	−0.05

Generally speaking, the people who are elected to the Singapore Parliament stop thinking about the public once they're elected. (R)	0.04	0.07*	0.04	0.04	0.06	0.02
Government officials pay little attention to what citizens like me think. (R)	0.07*	0.05	0.04	0.04	0.01	0.04
R^2	0.121***	0.073***	0.086***	0.074***	0.079***	0.076***

Notes:
* $p < 0.05$. ** $p < 0.01$. *** $p < 0.001$.
R = Reverse-coded statement. Values are standardized regression coefficients.

the rankings in terms of the respondents' satisfaction with certain democratic right. Singaporeans continued to be most dissatisfied with their right to criticize the government, freedom of speech and to gather and demonstrate.

Overall, with reference to Singaporeans' satisfaction with democratic rights, older respondents were less satisfied, with those between 70 and 79 years old recording the lowest mean scores for four out of six rights. Across the five rights that differed significantly across different age groups, respondents between the ages of 30 to 39 were most satisfied, with the highest mean scores in all five aspects. Respondents with higher education levels and higher household incomes were more satisfied with all six aspects of democratic rights.

There was a decline in the percentage of respondents who believed that voting constituted a citizen's duty compared to previous years. Nevertheless, the perceptions about whether their individual votes mattered remained unchanged from 2016; the majority of respondents disagreed that their votes did not matter. Respondents with higher education levels and higher household incomes were more likely to agree that they have a duty to vote. Skepticism regarding the impact of votes was most prominent among respondents between the ages of 20 and 49 years, male respondents and respondents with low and high household incomes.

With regard to the empowerment of voters, more respondents felt that they had the power to influence policymaking, and were more confident of their ability to make sense of Singapore's political landscape. Nevertheless, a detailed look into the different profiles of respondents revealed that younger respondents, respondents from lower income households, and respondents with lower education levels were still more likely to feel powerless in terms of their ability to influence government policies. With regard to their perceived ability to understand politics, respondents who are younger, female and single tended to be less confident.

Lastly, for the empathy and integrity of government officials, respondents in 2022 have become more skeptical. The 2022 QOL Survey results highlight a potential polarization of views with regard to corruption and the apathy of government officials in Singapore. Respondents between the ages of 30 and 39 years, and male, were more likely to perceive government officials to be corrupt and apathetic. Respondents with higher education levels were more likely to perceive that, once elected, government officials do not think about the public.

These perceptions and views about politics have an impact on Singaporeans' wellbeing. Except for the right to gather and demonstrate, satisfaction with all the other five democratic rights had a statistically significant and positive influence on satisfaction with life with Singaporeans' satisfaction with the right to criticize the government having the strongest influence. Unfortunately, they were also the least satisfied with this right. Satisfaction with the right to vote had the most impact on the affective components of wellbeing, while satisfaction with the right to gather and demonstrate had little influence. Citizens who felt they had a duty to vote and the power to influence government policy or actions had higher levels of wellbeing.

References

Bahry, D., & Silver, B. (1990). "Soviet citizen participation on the eve of democratization", *American Political Science Review, 84*(3), 821–848.

Barker, C., & Martin, B. (2011). "Participation: The happiness connection". *Regular Issue, 7*(1). https://doi.org/10.16997/jdd.120

Flavin, P., & Keane, M. (2012). "Life satisfaction and political participation: Evidence from the United States". *Journal of Happiness Studies, 13*(1), 63–78.

He, L., Wang, K., Liu, T., Li, T., & Zhu, B. (2022). "Does political participation help improve the life satisfaction of urban residents: Empirical evidence from China". *PLOS ONE, 17*(10). https://doi.org/10.1371/journal.pone.0273525

Hooghe, M., Hosch-Dayican, B., & van Deth, J. W. (2014). "Conceptualizing political participation". *Acta Politica, 49*(3), 337–348. https://doi.org/10.1057/ap.2014.7

Khoo, S. Z., Ho, L. H., Lee, E. H., Goh, D. K., Zhang, Z., Ng, S. H., Qi, H., & Shim, K. J. (2020). "Social media analytics: A case study of Singapore general election 2020". 2020 IEEE International Conference on Big Data (Big Data). https://doi.org/10.1109/bigdata50022.2020.9378358

Kwan, J. Y. (2022). "'Democracy and active citizenship are not just about the elections': Youth civic and political participation during and beyond Singapore's nine-day pandemic election (GE2020)". *YOUNG, 30*(3), 247–264. https://doi.org/10.1177/11033088211059595

Pirralha, A. (2017). "Political participation and wellbeing in the Netherlands: Exploring the causal links". *Applied Research in Quality of Life, 12*, 327–341.

Putnam, R. (2000). *Bowling alone: The collapse and revival of American community.* New York: Simon & Schuster.

Ruess, C., Hoffmann, C. P., Boulianne, S., & Heger, K. (2021). "Online political participation: The evolution of a concept". *Information, Communication & Society*, 1–18. https://doi.org/10.1080/13691 18x.2021.2013919

Shi, S., Zhang, Z., Yang, T., Wang, J., Li, T., Zhao, J., Liu, T., Wang, K., Yang, M., & He, L. (2022). "Is life satisfaction higher for citizens engaged in political participation: Analysis based on the Chinese Social Survey". *PLOS ONE, 17*(12). https://doi.org/10.1371/journal.pone.0279436

Sloam, J. (2016). "Diversity and voice: The political participation of young people in the European Union". *The British Journal of Politics and International Relations, 18*(3), 521–537. https://doi.org/10.1177/1369148116647176

Soon, C. (2015). "Study on internet and media use during general election 2015", presentation at the IPS Post-Election Conference 2015, 4 November 2015. http://lkyspp2.nus.edu.sg/ips/wp-content/uploads/sites/2/2015/10/S1_Carol-Soon_PEC_Media-Panel_041115.pdf

Soon, C., & Neo, Y.N. (2021). "The role of digital media in Singapore's general election 2020". *Southeast Asian Affairs 2021*, 313–332. https://doi.org/10.1355/9789814951753-018

Stutzer, A., & Frey, B. S. (2006). "Political participation and procedural utility: An empirical study". *European Journal of Political Research, 45*(3), 391–418. https://doi.org/10.1111/j.1475-6765.2006.00303.x

Tambyah, S. K., Tan, S. J., & Kau, A. K. (2010). *The wellbeing of Singaporeans: Values, lifestyles, satisfaction and quality of life.* Singapore: World Scientific Publishing Pte Ltd.

Tambyah, S. K., & Tan. S. J. (2013). *Happiness and wellbeing: The Singaporean experience.* London: Routledge.

Tambyah, S. K., & Tan, S. J. (2018). *Happiness, wellbeing and society: What matters for Singaporeans.* London: Routledge.

Tan, E. (2020, 15 September). *Despite Eld's lengthy statement on GE2020, some key questions remain unanswered.* TODAY. Retrieved 1 May 2023, from www.todayonline.com/commentary/despite-elds-lengthy-statement-ge2020-some-key-questions-remain-unanswered

Teo, K. K. (2021, 8 April). *Are Singaporeans really politically apathetic?* Lee Kuan Yew School of Public Policy. Retrieved 7 March 2023, from https://lkyspp.nus.edu.sg/ips/publications/details/are-singaporeans-really-politically-apathetic

Teorell, J. (2006). "Political Participation and three theories of democracy: a research inventory and agenda". *European Journal of Political Research, 45*, 787–810.

Theocharis, Y., & van Deth, J. (2018). *Political participation in a changing world: Conceptual and empirical challenges in the study of citizen engagement.* London: Routledge.

Veenhoven, R. (1988). "The utility of happiness". *Social Indicators Research, 20*(4), 333–354.

Verba, S., & Nie, N. (1972). *Participation in America.* New York: Harper and Row.

Vitak, J., Zube, P., Smock, A., Carr, C. T., Ellison, N., & Lampe, C. (2011). "It's complicated: Facebook users' political participation in the 2008 election". *Cyberpsychology, Behavior, and Social Networking, 14*(3), 107–114. https://doi.org/10.1089/cyber.2009.0226

Ward, G. (2019). *World happiness report 2019 chapter 3: Happiness and voting behaviour* (pp. 48–65). World Happiness Report.

Weitz-Shapiro, R., & Winters, M. S. (2011). "The link between voting and life satisfaction in Latin America". *Latin American Politics and Society, 53*(4), 101–126.

8 The impact of the COVID-19 pandemic on the wellbeing of Singaporeans

The COVID-19 pandemic has brought about unprecedented changes to people's lives. Singapore has gone through several waves of infection and multiple phases of lockdowns, deeply affecting various aspects of the daily lives of Singaporeans. In this chapter, we explore the impact of COVID-19 on the wellbeing of Singaporeans and the demographic segments that were particularly affected. Respondents were asked to reflect on the last two years of the pandemic (mid-2020 to mid-2022) as they answered the questions in the 2022 QOL Survey. Where applicable, we compared our findings with results of surveys and polls conducted during the same period. Specifically, we examine the impact of COVID-19 through four perspectives: (1) economic impact; (2) health risks; (3) familial factors and (4) social disruptions.

Singaporeans' concerns about the COVID-19 pandemic

First, we present an overview of Singaporeans' concerns about the COVID-19 pandemic from the responses to the eight statements shown in Figure 8.1. All respondents in the 2022 QOL Survey rated their agreement with each statement on a six-point scale (1 = Strongly disagree, 6 = Strongly agree). In general, Singaporeans were most concerned about the health risks related to COVID-19, and they were more worried for their family members than for themselves. Following the health risks, Singaporeans were worried about losing their jobs and suffered from disruptions to their social lives due to the pandemic. Finally, familial factors, such

DOI: 10.4324/9781003399650-8

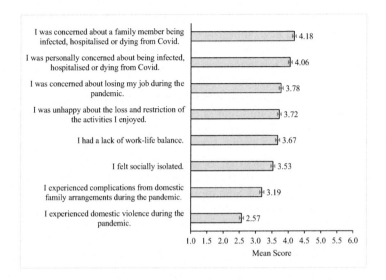

Figure 8.1 Singaporeans' concerns about COVID-19 (2022).

Note: Error bars represent 95 per cent confidence intervals. All items were rated on a six-point Likert scale (1 = Strongly disagree, 6 = Strongly agree).

as complications arising from domestic living arrangements and domestic violence, impacted Singaporeans the least.

Similar concerns about job security and health risks were reflected in an earlier survey of 500 respondents in July 2020. Unemployment rates and the state of the economy were found to be the biggest causes of anxiety, with 78 per cent of respondents highlighting the anxiety caused by economic uncertainty. Anxiety over health risks related to COVID-19 were also felt by 73 per cent of respondents, who indicated their worries over not knowing when they might contract the disease in public spaces, or what the ensuing long-term economic disruption might look like (Goh, 2020).

The economic impact of COVID-19

As noted in Figure 8.1, after the health risks, the third highest concern was about job loss. This economic impact was felt keenly by slightly more than a third (38.5 per cent) of the Singaporeans surveyed, who reported that someone in their household had lost income during the last two years and less than a third (27 per cent) managed to find new employment (Figure 8.2). About one in four Singaporeans (26.8 per cent) also expected someone in their household to lose their job in the next three to six months.

The economic impact of the pandemic was also examined in a September 2020 poll conducted by market research company Ipsos. They found that in comparison to respondents from five other Southeast Asian countries (Indonesia, Malaysia, the Philippines, Thailand and Vietnam), Singaporeans were most worried about job security. While an average of 49 per cent of respondents among all six countries indicated that they were worried, 56 per cent of Singaporean respondents were "less confident" about job security for themselves, their families, or other people they know personally. Singaporeans were also most pessimistic about an economic recovery (Lim, 2020). In another report released by Ministry of Trade and Industry (MTI) on 24 November 2021, the unemployment rate in Singapore had risen to an unprecedented level, with 113,500 jobs lost during Singapore's first Circuit Breaker (the equivalent of a lockdown) that took place between April and June 2020. Singapore's overall unemployment rate was 2.6 per cent, which was lower than that

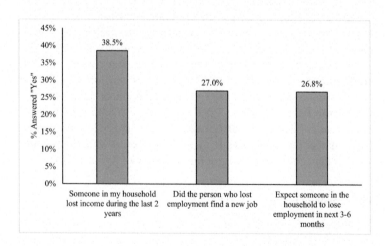

Figure 8.2 Employment and loss of income due to COVID-19 (2022).

of the United States (4.8 per cent), Hong Kong (4.5 per cent) and Germany (3.4 per cent). However, the COVID-19 pandemic brought about the greatest increase in employment figures compared to previous crises such as the dot-com bust and the Asian Financial Crisis (Tan, 2021).

To mitigate the economic disruptions caused by COVID-19, various forms of governmental support were provided. In 2020 and 2021, the Singapore government spent $72.3 billion on a variety of subsidies, grants and cash payouts (Tham, 2023). In 2020, five budgets were formulated with the aim of preserving jobs, helping businesses with cashflow and supporting Singaporean workers. Three budgets in 2021 were targeted at helping Singaporeans adapt to living with COVID-19 through restructuring and upskilling (Ministry of Finance Singapore, 2022).

To support lower- to middle-income employees and self-employed persons who had experienced involuntary job loss, the government introduced the COVID-19 Recovery Grant in January 2021. Originally stipulated to end in December 2021, the government extended the deadline twice, to 31 December 2023. This grant provided up to $700 per month for three months to lower- to middle-income employees and self-employed persons who had experienced involuntary job loss. Through this grant, Singapore's Ministry of Social and Family Development (MSF) has disbursed approximately $75 million, which supported 31,000 individuals as at November 2022 (Channel News Asia, 2022).

For lower-income households whose incomes have been directly affected by their contraction of COVID-19 or quarantine orders, the government also provided a one-time payout of up to $1,000 through the Courage Fund initiative, which officially ended on 24 November 2022. As of 14 February 2022, more than 6,600 individuals have benefitted from such payouts (Toh, 2021).

Given the disruption caused by the COVID-19 Safe Management Measures, the government also provided economic support to small businesses, notably hawkers and market stallholders. In February 2022, the Small Business Recovery Grant was announced, as part of a larger $500 million Jobs and Business Support Package. As of June 2022, more than 40,000 small businesses have received approximately $132 million from the government. The grant also provided eligible companies with a one-time cash support of $1,000 for each Singapore citizen or

Permanent Resident employee with mandatory Central Provident Fund contributions, capped at $10,000 per firm (Tan, 2022).

Health risks related to COVID-19

To assess the extent of Singaporeans' concerns with health risks, we collated the percentages of respondents who agreed to varying degrees to the statements about being infected with COVID-19. Responses were calibrated on a six-point Likert scale (1 = "strongly disagree" to 6 = "strongly agree"). As shown in Figure 8.3 below, a total of 72.5 per cent of respondents were personally concerned about being infected, hospitalized or dying from COVID-19 (31.1 per cent for "somewhat agree", 27.6 per cent for "agree" and 13.8 per cent for "strongly agree"). A total of 75.5 per cent of respondents expressed similar concerns for their family members (30.2 per cent for "somewhat agree", 29.1 per cent for "agree" and 16.2 per cent for "strongly agree").

The perceived health risks are a reflection of the fears and concerns regarding the infectious nature of COVID-19 and the strict social isolation measures that were put in place to contain the spread of the virus. In the early stages of the pandemic, patients who were hospitalized were unable to have physical contact

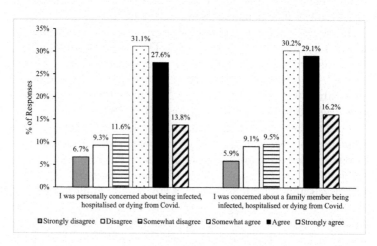

Figure 8.3 Health risks related to COVID-19 (2022).

with their family members, who may also be in isolation themselves. The initial period before the vaccine breakthrough also
saw patients spending their dying moments alone (Yong, 2021).
Under such circumstances, Singaporeans had been worried about
the health of their family members, especially young children and
elderly parents. Nevertheless, in comparison with respondents
from five other Southeast Asian countries (Indonesia, Malaysia,
the Philippines, Thailand and Vietnam), market research company Ipsos found that Singaporeans were the least worried about
contracting COVID-19 (Lim, 2020).

Impact on psychological health

The COVID-19 pandemic has had a significant impact on psychological health due to a range of stressors, such as the fear
of contracting the virus, social isolation, financial difficulties,
uncertainty about the future and changes in daily routines.
These stressors, if not properly managed, can lead to a long-
lasting impact on psychological health. Respondents of the
2022 QOL Survey were asked to complete an adapted version
of the 12-item General Health Questionnaire (GHQ-12), which
assesses various aspects of psychological wellbeing, including
self-confidence and feelings of depression. All items were rated
on a four-point Likert scale, with higher scores indicating *better*
psychological health.

As seen in Figure 8.4, Singaporeans have moderately acceptable levels of psychological health given that their scores were
above the mid-point of 2.5 on all 12 items. The item with the
lowest score – "Have you recently felt constantly under strain?" –
suggests that Singaporeans frequently felt stressed out and that
their psychological health was suffering from constant stress. The
next few aspects of psychological health that Singaporeans fared
the worst in included feeling unhappy, useless and depressed,
and being unable to enjoy their normal day-to-day activities. Our
findings are mirrored in a September 2021 poll commissioned by
the *Straits Times*. They discovered that mental health had declined
since the COVID-19 pandemic began, with 75 per cent of the
1,000 respondents noting that they felt sad or depressed, and 66
per cent feeling lonely. Similarly, a study by the Institute of Mental
Health reported that 13 per cent of the 1,058 Singaporeans and

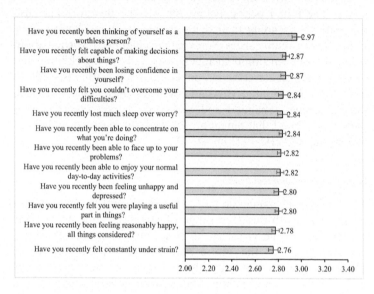

Figure 8.4 Mean scores of psychological wellbeing (2022).

Note: Scores ranged from 1 to 4, and higher scores indicate *better* psychological health. Error bars represent 95 per cent confidence intervals.

Permanent Residents polled experienced symptoms of anxiety or depression between May 2020 and June 2021 (Lai, 2022).

Sources of individual differences for health risks

As shown in Table 8.1, female Singaporeans were significantly more concerned about being personally infected by COVID-19 (mean of 4.15 out of a six-point scale) than male Singaporeans (3.84). Female Singaporeans were also significantly more concerned about family members being infected by COVID-19 (mean of 4.25) than male Singaporeans (4.07).

Statistically, more married Singaporeans were concerned about being personally infected by COVID-19 (mean of 4.15) than single Singaporeans (3.89). Singaporeans' concern about family members being infected by COVID-19 did not vary across marital status.

In general, for age, there was an inverted U-shape trend for concerns about personal COVID-19 infections, and the differences

Table 8.1 Sources of individual differences for health risks (2022)

Demographics	General Health	Personally concerned about being infected	Concerned about a family member being infected
Gender			
- Male	2.85	3.94	4.07
- Female	2.86	4.15	4.25
- F-stats	0.13	10.58	7.34
- *p*	0.716	< 0.001	0.007
Marital Status			
- Single	2.74	3.89	4.10
- Married	2.92	4.15	4.20
- F-stats	40.30	14.53	2.42
- *p*	< 0.001	< 0.001	0.120
Age			
- 20–29	2.67	3.92	4.29
- 30–39	2.75	4.31	4.38
- 40–49	2.81	4.22	4.35
- 50–59	3.00	3.93	3.93
- 60–69	2.99	3.90	4.01
- 70–79	3.03	3.68	3.41
- F-stats	18.78	6.74	11.46
- *p*	< 0.001	< 0.001	< 0.001
Education			
- Low	2.85	4.08	4.05
- Medium	2.89	3.97	4.09
- High	2.84	4.07	4.23
- F-stats	1.21	0.87	3.14
- *p*	0.298	0.421	0.044
Household Income			
- Low	2.74	3.85	3.84
- Medium-low	2.84	3.99	4.15
- Medium-high	2.89	4.12	4.23
- High	2.90	4.19	4.33
- F-stats	5.15	3.75	6.52
- *p*	0.002	0.011	< 0.001

were statistically significant. The younger Singaporeans (20–29 years) were the least concerned about being personally infected (mean of 3.92), those in the middle-age groups were most concerned (4.31 for 30–39 years and 4.22 for 40–49 years), while those in the older age groups were moderately concerned (3.93 for 50–59 years, 3.90 for 60–69 years and 3.68 for 70–79 years).

This inverted U-shaped trend was also observed for the concern about family members being infected with COVID-19. For instance, the younger Singaporeans (20–29 years) were the least concerned about family members being infected (mean of 4.29), those in the middle age groups were most concerned (4.38 for 30–39 years and 4.35 for 40–49 years), while those in the older age groups were moderately concerned (3.93 for 50–59 years, 4.01 for 60–69 years and 3.41 for the 70–79 years age group).

Singaporeans' concern about being personally infected by COVID-19 did not vary with education levels, but their concern about family members being infected by COVID-19 was statistically different across education levels. Those with low levels of education were less concerned about their family members being infected by COVID-19 (mean of 4.07) than those with high education levels (4.23).

Singaporeans' concern about personally being infected by COVID-19 differed significantly across household incomes. Those with low household income showed the least concern about personally infected by COVID-19 (mean of 3.85) versus those with high household income (4.19). This pattern of response also applies to the concern about family members being infected. Those with low household income showed the least concern (mean of 3.84) versus those with high household income (4.33).

Familial factors

As shown in Figure 8.5, Singaporeans generally suffered minimal familial disruptions from COVID-19. A six-point Likert scale was used (1 = "strongly disagree" to 6 = "strongly agree"). Less than two in ten (18 per cent) Singaporeans strongly disagreed and less than one in ten (6.7 per cent) strongly agreed that they had such complications. More than a third (39.9 per cent) disagreed or somewhat disagreed that they experienced such complications, while a third (35.3 per cent) somewhat agreed or agreed about such

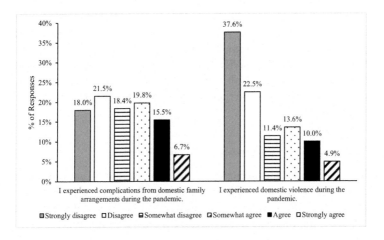

Figure 8.5 Familial factors related to COVID-19 (2022).

complications. Fortunately, the majority of Singaporeans (71.5 per cent) strongly disagreed, disagreed or somewhat disagreed that they experienced domestic violence during the pandemic. Nevertheless, it was disconcerting that there were Singaporeans (28.5 per cent) who reported that they experienced domestic violence during the pandemic.

Our findings related to familial factors echoed similar concerns about domestic violence and the impact on mental wellbeing during the onset of the pandemic lockdowns. In May 2020, shortly after the onset of COVID-19 and in the midst of Singapore's first Circuit Breaker, the police noted that family violence reports rose by 22 per cent, with offences including the use of criminal force, assault and criminal intimidation. Calls to the mental health related hotlines have also increased (Lau, 2021; Yong, 2021). During the Circuit Breaker, Singaporeans were mandated to stay within the confines of their living spaces unless there was a need to head out. Thus, families who did not have a "strong dynamic" or were in "pressure cooker environments" would invariably experience higher potential for family violence episodes (Yong, 2021).

With the increase in episodes of family violence, COVID-19 has also brought to the fore conversations surrounding mental health, which has traditionally been issues that Singaporeans shy away from (Yong, 2021). In February 2021, an inter-agency task force was set up to raise awareness on family violence and brainstorm for solutions to help victims. Accordingly, as of December 2021, all police land divisions have begun the initiative of referring family violence offenders to social workers, who would assess if further intervention and help is necessary (Lau, 2021).

Sources of individual differences for familial factors

Male Singaporeans were more affected by complications from domestic family arrangements (mean of 3.25) and domestic violence (2.72) than female Singaporeans (3.03 for complications arising from domestic family arrangements; 2.31 for domestic violence) (see Figure 8.6).

Married Singaporeans were also more affected by complications arising from family arrangements (mean of 3.22) and domestic violence (2.61) than single Singaporeans (3.01 for complications arising from family arrangements, and 2.34 for domestic violence) (see Table 8.2).

Age-wise, Singaporeans who were below 50 years were more affected by complications than those aged 50 years and above. For

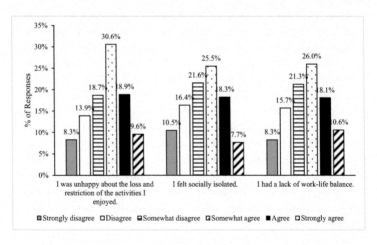

Figure 8.6 Social disruptions from COVID-19 (2022).

Table 8.2 Sources of individual differences for familial factors (2022)

Demographics	Experienced complications from domestic family arrangements	Experienced domestic violence
Gender		
- Male	3.25	2.72
- Female	3.03	2.31
- F-stats	9.40	31.03
- p	0.002	< 0.001
Marital Status		
- Single	3.01	2.34
- Married	3.22	2.61
- F-stats	8.13	12.60
- p	0.004	< 0.001
Age		
- 20–29	3.30	2.71
- 30–39	3.62	3.00
- 40–49	3.34	2.66
- 50–59	2.76	2.17
- 60–69	2.71	2.03
- 70–79	2.71	2.06
- F-stats	20.96	20.64
- p	< 0.001	< 0.001
Education		
- Low	3.03	2.57
- Medium	2.91	2.31
- High	3.27	2.56
- F-stats	9.89	4.54
- p	< 0.001	0.011
Household Income		
- Low	3.03	2.32
- Medium-low	3.00	2.37
- Medium-high	3.22	2.63
- High	3.32	2.68
- F-stats	3.96	5.24
- p	0.008	0.001

instance, Singaporeans aged 30 to 39 years reported the highest mean of 3.62 about experiencing complications from domestic family arrangements, compared to those aged 60 to 69 years and 70 to 79 years who both reported the lowest mean of 2.71. This pattern of response was repeated in terms of domestic violence. Singaporeans aged below 50 years experienced more domestic violence than those aged 50 years and above. For instance, Singaporean aged 30 to 39 years reported the highest mean of 3.00 about experiencing domestic violence, compared to those aged 60 to 69 years who reported the lowest mean of 2.03.

Unfortunately, being better educated did not help Singaporeans in mitigating complications arising from domestic family arrangements. Singaporeans with low education and those with high education appeared to be equally affected by complications arising from domestic family arrangements (3.03 for low education and the highest mean of 3.27 for high education), compared to those with medium education (2.91). Singaporeans with low and high education were similarly affected by domestic violence during the pandemic (means of 2.57 and 2.56, respectively), compared to those with medium education (2.31).

Singaporeans who were in higher household income groups were more affected by complications arising from domestic family arrangements and domestic violence. Those with low and medium-low household incomes reported lower and lowest means of 3.03 and 3.00, respectively, on complications arising from domestic family arrangements, while those with medium-high and high household incomes reported the highest mean of 3.22 each. Singaporeans with low household income also reported the lowest mean of 2.32 on experience with domestic violence, while those with high household incomes reported the highest mean of 2.68.

Social disruptions from COVID-19

Singaporeans had to grapple with various social disruptions during the pandemic. Close to six out of ten Singaporeans (59.1 per cent) were unhappy about the loss and restrictions of the activities that they enjoyed. Five out of ten Singaporeans (51.5 per cent) felt they were socially isolated, while close to five out of ten (49.3 per cent) of Singaporeans reported a lack of work–life balance. These social disruptions are part of a larger social phenomenon described as "pandemic fatigue". This is characterized as "a feeling of exhaustion from the changes that the pandemic has brought about, as well as feeling a sense of dread and irritation with the constant news of the pandemic" (Abdullah, 2021). Attesting to the serious toll the pandemic has taken on mental health, a majority of Singaporeans polled between 2020 and 2021 reported feeling sad, depressed, lonely and anxious (Lai, 2022). Regarding the lack of work–life balance, the work from home (WFH) policy implemented by numerous companies during the COVID-19 pandemic has affected individuals living in smaller homes, since they are less able to "distinguish between home and office" (Yong, 2021). In the period prior to COVID-19, where only 6.2 per cent of firms in 2017 allowed their staff to work from home permanently, employers have now recognized that people can be trusted to work from home, with some workers being even more productive at home. Given that flexible work arrangements would likely become a permanent fixture even after the pandemic, the lack of work–life balance caused by workers' inability to carve out a designated office space for work in their homes is a problem that has to be addressed (Lai, 2022).

Sources of individual differences for social disruptions

There were no significant differences noted for gender and marital status (see Table 8.3). However, Singaporeans who were 30 to 39 years were the most unhappy about the loss and restriction of enjoyed activities (mean of 4.05), felt socially isolated the most (3.91) and were the most affected by a lack of work-life balance (4.02). Meanwhile, those in the 70 to 79 years age group were the least unhappy about the loss and restriction of enjoyed activities (3.15), felt the least socially isolated (2.94) and were least affected by lack of work–life balance (3.03).

Education-wise, there was a significant positive linear trend about the social disruptions of COVID-19. Singaporeans with high education were most unhappy about the loss and restriction of enjoyed activities (mean of 3.80) and were the most affected by lack of work–life balance (3.74). Singaporeans with low education were the least unhappy about the loss and restriction of enjoyed activities (3.37) and were the least affected by a lack of work–life balance (3.43).

Table 8.3 Sources of individual differences for social disruptions (2022)

Demographics	Unhappy about loss and restriction of activities enjoyed	Felt socially isolated	Lack of work-life balance
Gender			
- Male	3.74	3.55	3.71
- Female	3.60	3.41	3.53
- F-stats	4.52	4.45	7.81
- *p*	0.034	0.035	0.005
Marital Status			
- Single	3.66	3.44	3.60
- Married	3.68	3.50	3.63
- F-stats	0.09	0.77	0.28
- *p*	0.767	0.380	0.597
Age			
- 20–29	3.98	3.82	3.89
- 30–39	4.05	3.91	4.02
- 40–49	3.80	3.54	3.78
- 50–59	3.21	3.07	3.33
- 60–69	3.41	3.16	3.16
- 70–79	3.15	2.94	3.03
- F-stats	22.70	23.09	22.17
- *p*	< 0.001	< 0.001	< 0.001
Education			
- Low	3.37	3.38	3.43
- Medium	3.61	3.38	3.49
- High	3.80	3.55	3.74
- F-stats	12.88	3.14	8.57
- *p*	< .001	.044	< .001
Household Income			
- Low	3.26	3.34	3.42
- Medium-low	3.61	3.41	3.53
- Medium-high	3.76	3.51	3.73
- High	3.95	3.66	3.73
- F-stats	12.50	2.87	4.28
- *p*	< 0.001	0.035	0.005

There was also a significant positive linear trend for household income related to the social disruptions of COVID-19. Singaporeans with high household incomes were the most unhappy about the loss and restriction of enjoyed activities (mean of 3.95), felt the most socially isolated (3.66) and were the most affected by a lack of work–life balance (3.73). Singaporeans with low household incomes were the least unhappy about the loss and restriction of enjoyed activities (3.26), felt the least socially isolated (3.34) and were the least affected by a lack of work–life balance (3.42).

Trust for postpandemic times

Singaporeans had a high level of trust in the government's ability to navigate and lead Singapore in a postpandemic world. Close to two thirds (63.3 per cent) of Singaporeans surveyed responded "yes" when asked about this issue. Similarly, close to two thirds (64.3 per cent) of Singaporeans said "yes" when responding to the question about trusting their fellow Singaporeans to remain united in the face of future challenges. These percentages are in sharp contrast to the lower percentages for generalized trust (whether people can be trusted and would be fair or helpful), as seen in Figure 8.7. It is interesting to note Singaporeans are more trusting of the government and fellow citizens for a post-pandemic scenario compared to general day-to-day scenarios.

Similar to the results obtained in the 2022 QOL Survey, a study conducted by marketing research company Ipsos between May to June 2022 found that 74 per cent of Singaporeans were confident about the COVID-19 situation, which was comparatively higher than the average of 71 per cent gathered from respondents in Indonesia, Malaysia, the Philippines, Thailand and Vietnam (Ipsos, 2022). A study conducted by IPS also found that 65 per cent of respondents trusted that the government would be able to navigate and lead Singapore through the postpandemic world (Mathews et al., 2021). This could be related to the high satisfaction among Singaporeans regarding the government's overall handling of the pandemic. However, the survey also discovered that more than 50 per cent of respondents felt that Singaporeans were "too dependent on the government to help them overcome the economic problems related to COVID-19".

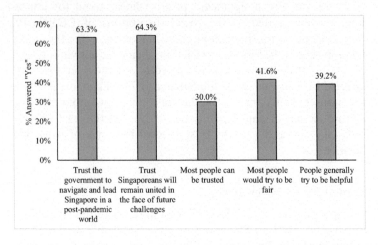

Figure 8.7 Trust for postpandemic times and generalized trust (2022).

In the same study by IPS, Singaporeans also expressed a high level of trust toward fellow citizens, with at least 70 per cent of respondents trusting that "Singaporeans would remain united in the face of future challenges". Additionally, at least 60 per cent of respondents trusted fellow citizens to continue observing COVID-19 measures both at home and outside.

The online poll released by the Ministry of Communications and Information on 19 March 2023 discovered that responses reflected higher levels of trust between citizens and the government, as well as trust among citizens. Respondents were generally confident of Singapore's ability to manage future pandemics well, with 75 per cent of the general population "strongly agree[ing]" or "agree[ing]" that Singapore would get through. Compared to the general population, where only 7 per cent expressed low confidence in Singapore's ability to face a future pandemic, 16 per cent of unemployed respondents expressed such sentiments. When asked to compare the strength of interpersonal relationships in 2019 and today, 77 per cent of respondents noted that family relationships grew stronger or remained constant. 82 per cent reported the same regarding relationships with their neighbors, while 71 per cent expressed such sentiments regarding friendships (Ministry of Communications and Information, 2023). Similar surveys conducted by Pew Research Centre and Edelman Trust Institute also reflected Singaporeans' high trust in the government, demonstrated by their willingness to cooperate with COVID-19 measures (Wong, 2023).

Sources of individual differences for trust for postpandemic times

Some demographic differences in trust were observed. While Singaporeans' trust in the government and other Singaporeans did not differ by marital status and education levels, there were notable differences by gender, household incomes and age.

As shown in Figures 8.8 and 8.9, more female than male Singaporeans had trust in the government's ability to navigate and lead Singapore in a postpandemic world (77.1 per cent for females versus 68.2 per cent for males), and trusted their fellow Singaporeans to remain united in the face of future challenges (76.7 per cent for females versus 70.2 per cent for males).

Singaporeans in the low and low-medium household income groups (see Figures 8.9 and 8.10) reported the lowest percentages

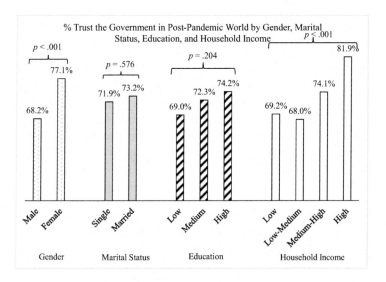

Figure 8.8 Trust in government by gender, marital status, education level and household income (2022).

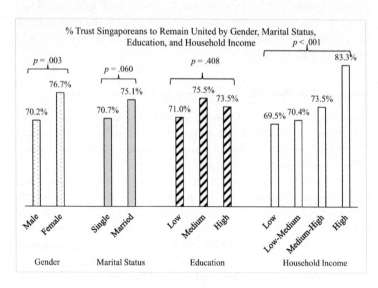

Figure 8.9 Trust in Singaporeans by gender, marital status, education level and household income (2022).

who trusted the government's ability to navigate and lead Singapore in a postpandemic world (69.3 per cent and 68 per cent, respectively), while those in the high household income group reported the highest percentage (81.9 per cent). This pattern of response was repeated for the trust in fellow Singaporeans to remain united in the face of future challenges. The lowest percentage (69.5 per cent) among the low household income group versus highest percentage (83.3 per cent) among the high household income group.

Finally, as shown in Figure 8.10, a clear inverted U-shape trend can be observed across different age groups. For instance, about seven out of ten (74.3 per cent) of younger Singaporeans in the 20 to 29 years age group trusted the government's ability to navigate and lead Singapore in a postpandemic world. This proportion decreased to the lowest of about six out of ten (66.4 per cent) among Singaporeans in the 40 to 49 years age group, before increasing to a high of more than eight out of ten (85.5 per cent) among the oldest age group (70–79 years).

This pattern of response is repeated for Singaporeans' trust in fellow Singaporeans to remain united in the face of future challenges. For instance, about seven out of ten (73.0 per cent)

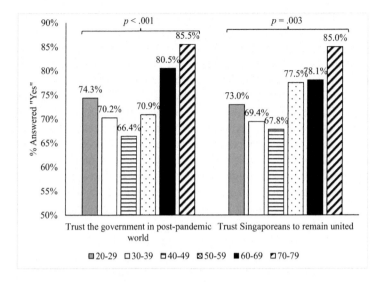

Figure 8.10 Age differences in trust (2022).

of younger Singaporeans in the 20 to 29 years age group trusted their fellow Singaporeans to remain united in the face of future challenges. This proportion decreased to the lowest of about six out of ten (67.8 per cent) among Singaporeans in the 40 to 49 years age group, before increasing to a high of more than eight out of ten (85 per cent) among the oldest age group (70–79 years).

Conclusion

This chapter has explored the impact of COVID-19 on Singaporeans' wellbeing in terms of economic impact, health risks, familial factors and social disruptions. The 2022 QOL Survey showed that health risks weighed most heavily on the minds of Singaporeans, followed by job security. Familial disruptions arising partly due to the changes in living arrangements caused by COVID-19 impacted Singaporeans the least.

While the Singapore government has introduced various schemes to mitigate financial disruptions caused by the closure of borders and lockdowns, Singaporeans were most worried about their job security and most pessimistic about economic recovery in comparison to respondents from five other Southeast Asian states. Pertaining to the health risks associated with COVID-19, the 2022 QOL Survey has revealed that Singaporeans were most worried about themselves or their loved ones contracting COVID-19. Nevertheless, they were least worried about the health risks associated with COVID-19 when compared to results from surveys on respondents from five other Southeast Asian states. While familial disruptions weighed least on the minds of Singaporeans, there was still a disconcerting percentage (28.5 per cent) of survey respondents who reported experiences of domestic violence, arising largely as a result of the extended periods of lockdowns. The pandemic also brought about social disruptions, such as the decline in mental wellbeing of Singaporeans caused by social isolation, lack of work–life balancing, feelings of uncertainty and pandemic fatigue.

Setting aside the various sources of stressors attributed to the pandemic, Singaporeans reported a high level of trust in the government's ability to navigate and lead Singapore in the postpandemic world (63.3 per cent). Singaporeans also reported a high level of trust (64.3 per cent) that fellow citizens would remain united and continue to observe COVID-19 measures.

References

Abdullah, A. Z. (2021, 19 May). *Guarding against pandemic fatigue in Singapore's COVID-19 Fight*. CNA. Retrieved 22 April 2023, from www.channelnewsasia.com/singapore/guarding-against-pandemic-fatigue-in-singapore-covid-19-fight-1382751

Channel News Asia. (2022, 16 December). *Covid-19 Recovery Grant extended by another year to end-2023*. Retrieved 22 April 2023, from www.channelnewsasia.com/singapore/covid-19-recovery-grant-application-period-extended-end-2023-msf-3146791

Goh, T. (2020, 24 September). *74% of Singaporeans and PRS feel anxious over pandemic impact: Study*. The Straits Times. Retrieved 22 April 2023, from www.straitstimes.com/singapore/health/74-of-singaporeans-and-prs-feel-anxious-over-pandemic-impact-study

Ipsos. (2022, 30 August). *Pandemic concerns recede, while rising prices drive value-driven purchases across SE Asia*. Ipsos News. Retrieved 22 April 2023, from www.ipsos.com/en-sg/pandemic-concerns-recede-while-rising-prices-drive-value-driven-purchases-across-se-asia

Lai, L. (2022, 7 May). *How Covid-19 changed the way we live, work and shop in Singapore*. The Straits Times. Retrieved 22 April 2023, from www.straitstimes.com/singapore/community/covid-19s-indelible-marks-on-mental-health-work-and-leisure

Lau, J. (2021, 8 December). *Coronavirus: More cases of family violence during circuit breaker; police to proactively help victims.* The Straits Times. Retrieved 22 April 2023, from www.straitstimes.com/singapore/courts-crime/coronavirus-more-cases-of-family-violence-during-circuit-breaker-police-to

Lim, M. Z. (2020, 24 October). *S'poreans least worried among S-E Asians about getting Covid-19, but less secure about jobs: Poll.* The Straits Times. Retrieved 22 April 2023, from www.straitstimes.com/singapore/singaporeans-least-worried-about-getting-covid-19-in-south-east-asia-but-less-confident-of

Mathews, M., Suhaini, S., Hou, M., & Tan, A. (2021). (working paper). *THE COVID-19 pandemic in Singapore, one year on: Population attitudes and sentiments.* Retrieved 22 April 2023, from https://lkyspp.nus.edu.sg/docs/default-source/ips/working-paper-40_the-covid-19-pandemic-in-singapore-one-year-on-population-attitudes-and-sentiments.pdf.

Ministry of Communications and Information. (2023). *Poll by MCI finds 7 in 10 Singapore residents positive about their overall quality of life post-pandemic.* Retrieved 22 April 2023, from www.mci.gov.sg/pressroom/news-and-stories/pressroom/2023/3/poll-by-mci-finds-7-in-10-singapore-residents-positive-about-their-overall-quality-of-life-post-pandemic

Ministry of Finance Singapore. (2022, 17 February). *COVID-19 measures enabled Singapore to mitigate short-term impact and prevent longer-term economic scarring.* Press Release. Retrieved 22 April 2023, from www.mof.gov.sg/news-publications/press-releases/covid-19-measures-enabled-singapore-to-mitigate-short-term-impact-and-prevent-longer-term-economic-scarring

Tan, A. (2022, 27 June). *More than 40,000 small businesses affected by Covid-19 measures receive $132m in cash support.* The Straits Times. Retrieved 22 April 2023, from www.straitstimes.com/business/companies-markets/more-than-40000-small-businesses-affected-by-covid-19-measures-receive-132m-in-cash-support

Tan, S.-A. (2021, 24 November). *Covid-19 drove unprecedented drop of 196,400 in S'pore employment; services hardest-hit: MTI report.* The Straits Times. Retrieved 22 April 2023, from www.straitstimes.com/singapore/jobs/covid-19-drove-unprecedented-drop-of-196400-in-singapore-employment-services-hardest

Tham, Y.-C. (2023, 18 January). *Govt should review $72.3B in Covid-19 spending for any payment errors: Watchdog.* The Straits Times. Retrieved 22 April 2023, from www.straitstimes.com/singapore/politics/government-should-review-723-billion-in-covid-19-spending-for-any-payment-errors-says-public-sector-accounts-watchdog

Toh, T. W. (2021, 1 August). *Lower-income S'pore households affected by Covid-19 to get more financial support*. The Straits Times. Retrieved 22 April 2023, from www.straitstimes.com/singapore/lower-income-hou seholds-affected-by-covid-19-to-get-more-financial-support

Wong, L. (2023, 24 March). *Opening speech by DPM Lawrence Wong at the debate on the motion on Singapore's response to Covid-19 (March 2023)*. Prime Minister's Office Singapore. Retrieved 22 April 2023, from www.pmo.gov.sg/Newsroom/DPM-Lawrence-Wong-at-the-Deb ate-on-the-Motion-on-Singapore-Response-to-COVID-Mar-2023

Yong, M. (2021, 23 January). *In focus: How a year of Covid-19 changed Singapore Forever*. Channel News Asia. Retrieved 22 April 2023, from www.channelnewsasia.com/singapore/covid-19-pandemic-singapore-one-year-on-coronavirus-419301

9   Conclusion

In this concluding chapter, we collate and discuss some of the key insights of the 2022 QOL Survey, and reflect on how connecting the various findings may provide a holistic perspective of happiness and wellbeing in Singapore. In the previous chapters, we have covered a wide range of topics including satisfaction with life and life domains, happiness, enjoyment, achievement, control, purpose, psychological flourishing, the income-happiness equation, economic wellbeing, personal values, value orientations, satisfaction with democratic rights, views on politics and the impact of the COVID-19 pandemic on the wellbeing of Singaporeans. We conducted demographic analyses and showed how perceptions of wellbeing varied across age, education, gender, marital status and household income. Where applicable, we conducted longitudinal comparisons of the 2022 QOL Survey data with previous datasets from the 2016 QOL Survey (Tambyah & Tan, 2018) and the 2011 QOL Survey (Tambyah & Tan, 2013) and noted the variations and trends over the years. In addition, we examined the impact of personal values, satisfaction with democratic rights and views on politics on wellbeing outcomes such as satisfaction with life, satisfaction with life domains, the Cantril Ladder, the overall quality of life, happiness, enjoyment, achievement, control and purpose. In the sections to follow, we will begin with a note on the economic, social and political climate of the 2022 QOL Survey, followed by the discussion on some of the key findings on wellbeing outcomes, the effects of demographics on wellbeing outcomes, values and wellbeing, the clusters of Singaporeans and the impact of the

DOI: 10.4324/9781003399650-9

COVID-19 pandemic on the wellbeing of Singaporeans. We end the chapter with directives for future research.

The economic, social and political climate of the 2022 QOL Survey

The 2022 QOL Survey was conducted between 23 June 2022 and 25 July 2022 during an uncertain economic, social and political climate. Singapore, like many other countries, was at the tail end of a long and exhausting battle with the COVID-19 pandemic. There were intermittent fears of recession and high unemployment amid a global economic slowdown due to the pandemic. Paradoxically, there were also inflationary pressures with costs of living rising at alarming rates. The Russia–Ukraine War, which started on 24 February 2022, brought about further disruptions to global supply chains. As a nation that is reliant on global connections and trade, Singapore has been grappling with various economic and social challenges due to these geopolitical changes and tensions.

On the political front, the most recent election in Singapore was the 2020 General Election (GE2020) which was conducted under the cloud of the COVID-19 pandemic. Instead of the door-to-door visits and evening rallies at stadiums and open fields, which drew large crowds, political parties pivoted to online rallies and relied heavily on social media for campaigning. The People's Action Party (PAP) positioned itself as the government that could be trusted to help Singaporeans weather the ups and downs of the pandemic and introduced numerous financial initiatives to help individuals, families and businesses. The PAP garnered 61.24 per cent of the votes (compared to 69.9 per cent in 2016) and won 83 seats out of 93 available seats. However, another "Group Representative Constituency" (GRC), which is a mega-conglomeration of five constituencies, was lost to the Workers' Party which had a strong showing in GE2020.

Key findings on wellbeing outcomes

At first glance, the overall picture on the wellbeing of Singaporeans seemed to be a somber one with scores on many wellbeing outcomes slipping from previous years. However, there is a silver lining to some of these dark clouds. These findings could offer insights into what matters for the wellbeing of Singaporeans and highlight opportunities to improve this sense of wellbeing.

As suggested by research studies in this arena, economic prosperity (e.g., higher GDP and household incomes) would likely have a positive effect on wellbeing. Singapore's per capita GDP has been rising from S$63,050 (2011) to S$73,167 in (2016) and now S$114,165 (2022). Similarly, the average median household income has improved from S$8,722 (2011) to S$10,336 (2016) and now S$9,520 (2021) and S$10,099 (2022). However, Singaporeans' perceptions and assessments of their wellbeing have not improved correspondingly.

With regard to the cognitive aspects of wellbeing, there were three different assessments of life satisfaction that were used in the 2022 OQL Survey. In terms of satisfaction with life, the composite mean score for 2022 (3.92) fell behind 2016 (4.29), and the individual mean scores were also lower in 2022. In terms of satisfaction with life domains, all the mean scores for 2022 were below those of 2016. Nonetheless, all the mean scores in 2022 were above four (on a six-point scale) and in the "satisfied" spectrum. Singaporeans' Cantril Ladder scores slipped a bit from the 2016 QOL Survey. However, Singaporeans still evaluated their current lives fairly positively (5.99, 6th rung on the Cantril Ladder) and remained optimistic about their lives five years into the future (6.45).

For the affective aspects of wellbeing, we used indicators related to happiness, enjoyment, achievement, control and purpose and a Flourishing Scale (for psychological flourishing). Over the past ten years (2011 to 2022), Singaporeans have become less happy, enjoyed life less and have felt a decreased sense of achievement. Compared to 2016, most Singaporeans felt they did not have control over their lives and a sense of purpose. Singaporeans had declined in their psychological flourishing over the past decade.

What are some possible reasons for these key findings? First, there seems to be a manifestation of the Easterlin Paradox where increased incomes did not lead to increased happiness. This was also observed in the results from the 2016 QOL Survey when we started having a closer look at the income-happiness equation. Suppressed levels of wellbeing despite economic prosperity could be due to the effects of social comparisons and rising aspirations in a competitive and achievement-oriented society like Singapore. Second, the low levels of wellbeing reported could be attributed to the COVID-19 pandemic. As noted in the 2021–2022 Human Development Index (HDI) Report, "while HDI tends to trend upward globally over time, more than 90% of the 191 countries analyzed for the 2021/22 HDI report suffered a decline in overall HDI in either 2020 or 2021" (United Nations Development Programme, 2022). The World Happiness Reports in 2021, 2022 and 2023 also flagged increasing rates of anxiety, depression and sadness as many countries grappled with the economic and social repercussions of the pandemic.

The effect of demographics on wellbeing outcomes

For the 2022 QOL Survey, we noted individual differences for different demographic groups for the various wellbeing outcomes. While these sources of individual differences provided additional insights, care should be taken in interpreting some of the results as the correlations were generally small (which is common in social sciences studies of this nature). We provide an overview of a selection of key demographic differences with some implications from these findings.

Gender

For the cognitive aspects of wellbeing, a gender effect was observed only for the Cantril Ladder scores. Males rated their current lives to be significantly better than females, although both genders expected similar scores on the Cantril Ladder in five years' time. Female Singaporeans were less satisfied with their household incomes and health. Males scored significantly higher on all aspects of affective wellbeing than females. Compared to 2016, the gender effect in 2022 was more pronounced. This implied that female Singaporeans may not have access to the opportunities to be satisfied with their lives and life domains and to have more favorable perceptions of the affective aspects of wellbeing. The government and civil society in Singapore have been aware of the issues related to gender equality. In the past year, a white paper on gender equality has spawned debates on ensuring opportunities for all citizens regardless of gender and to eradicate barriers to gender equality in the home, workplaces and other spaces in society (Ministry of Social and Family Development Singapore, 2022).

Marital status

Being married seemed to have some impact on several wellbeing outcomes. For instance, married Singaporeans perceived their lives to be better now, and in five years' time. Married respondents also reported greater happiness, enjoyment, achievement, control, purpose and psychological flourishing than the singles. As we noted in the earlier chapters, marriage offers an opportunity for individuals to pool their financial resources and this might be helpful in meeting various needs such as housing. Unfortunately, in Singapore, singles face several disadvantages in terms of housing, as more affordable public housing options with government subsidies are accessible primarily for married couples (Ng, 2023; The Workers' Party, 2022; Zachariah, 2023).

Age

The impact of age on wellbeing outcomes was varied. Our discussion was mainly on older versus younger respondents when differences were noted instead of detailed comparisons across the various age groups. For instance, younger people (20 to 29 years) felt bad about their current lives but were more optimistic about their future lives. In contrast, older Singaporeans felt better now, but they expected their lives to deteriorate in five years' time. As Singaporeans got older, they tended to be happier, enjoyed life more, felt they had accomplished more, had more control, and had a stronger sense of purpose. Those between the ages of 60 and 69 years had the lowest psychological flourishing scores, while respondents in the 30 to 39 years age group had the highest psychological flourishing scores. Psychological flourishing of the other age groups fell in between the scores of those aged 30 to 39 years and 60 to 69 years. With Singapore's ageing population, there will be challenges ahead in terms of helping older Singaporeans to age well. It is encouraging to note that there are already many government and civil society initiatives in place such as the 2023 Action Plan for Successful Ageing by the Ministry of Health (Ministry of Health Singapore, 2023). More research on the wellbeing of older Singaporeans would also be helpful to provide a deeper understanding of the needs of older Singaporeans.

Education and household income

Education contributed to more differentiation in wellbeing outcomes. Education was positively correlated with all five aspects of affective wellbeing and psychological flourishing. Like education, household income had an important impact on various wellbeing outcomes. Household income had some impact on Singaporeans' wellbeing outcomes in terms of life satisfaction (Chapter 2). Generally, respondents with higher incomes also had higher means on the wellbeing outcomes of happiness, enjoyment, achievement, control, purpose and psychological flourishing (Chapter 3). The effect of household income was more thoroughly examined in Chapter 4. In that chapter, we noted the upward trending patterns correlating household income with the wellbeing outcomes. However, those with the highest household incomes might not be the happiest or most satisfied. In terms of economic wellbeing, our analyses confirmed that satisfaction with household income (i.e., financial satisfaction) and satisfaction with standard of living were positively associated with the wellbeing indicators.

The greater importance of Singaporeans' perceptions of their socio-economic status over actual income is also evident from their correlations with the wellbeing outcomes. While household income had weak to moderate correlations with affective and cognitive aspects of wellbeing, Singaporeans' satisfaction with their household income had moderate to strong correlations with wellbeing. Thus, we can surmise that satisfaction with one's socioeconomic status is an important driver of economic wellbeing, and not necessarily the particular levels of income although those with higher household incomes were more financially comfortable. Nonetheless, "happiness equality" due to education and income is a somewhat worrying trend if only the better educated and rich have a better sense of wellbeing.

Values and wellbeing

Values play a prominent role in Singaporeans' wellbeing. In the 2022 QOL Survey, we examined the influence of two broad types of values on wellbeing. We adopted the LOV to assess the importance of certain personal values to Singaporeans. Beyond personal strivings, we also examined value orientations on a broader scale with regard to four major aspects of life (i.e., family values, tradition, sustainability and materialism).

With regard to personal strivings, there were no significant shifts in the importance ranking of items in the LOV over the past three QOL Surveys (2011, 2016 and 2022), with security and self-respect continuing to be the top two values for Singaporeans, while the values of fun and enjoyment and excitement continued to be of lower or lowest importance. There was a definitive negative trend for all nine values of the LOV in the 2022 QOL Survey when compared to the 2011 and 2016 QOL Surveys. This decrease in importance across all the values may signify that Singaporeans are experiencing a global shift in what they value in life. Perhaps there are certain values that are more pertinent to Singaporeans in the Asian context that are not reflected in the LOV. For instance, with the COVID-19 pandemic claiming more than 1,400 lives in Singapore by June 2022 (Ministry of Health Singapore, 2022), Singaporeans may care more about their family members given the unpredictable nature of COVID-19. With the looming climate change crisis, Singaporeans may also reorient themselves to hold the value of sustainability more closely to heart than the personal values measured in the LOV.

It was interesting to note that, on the whole, Singaporeans did not place much importance on the value of excitement. However, this value featured significantly in making Singaporeans happier, enjoy life more, have a greater sense of achievement, as well as perceive greater control and purpose in their lives. Similarly, we noted that the lowest ranked value of excitement also positively and significantly influenced Singaporeans' satisfaction with life. This suggests that Singaporeans may not be aware that they are neglecting important aspects of their lives that are crucial to happiness (e.g., excitement), while they incessantly pursue other values (e.g., security and self-respect) that have little incremental influence on their wellbeing.

One plausible reason for these seemingly contradictory results is that Singaporeans may not like to openly admit in a survey setting that they place a high importance on "nonproductive" values such as fun and enjoyment and excitement. However, our correlational analyses showed that these values do play an important part in ensuring Singaporeans' cognitive and affective wellbeing. Notably, Singaporeans who are better educated and have higher incomes placed a greater emphasis on such "nonproductive" values. Perhaps better education and higher income have been achieved at the expense of having more leisure time, potentially explaining the heightened appreciation of fun and enjoyment and excitement among the more financially well-off Singaporeans. This indicates that to survive and thrive in a fast moving and technology-driven world, subconsciously, Singaporeans may have realized that they need to have some fun and enjoyment to relieve the stresses of everyday life and to complement the pursuit of other life goals.

Clusters of Singaporeans

We adopted a segmentation approach for our examination of the four broad value orientations. Similar to the past two QOL Surveys (2011 and 2016), this set of value orientations in the 2022 QOL Survey included statements relating to family values, sustainability, traditionalism and materialism, which are distinct from the LOV. The number of clusters have changed from a six-cluster solution in 2011, to a five-cluster solution in 2016 and now to a four-cluster solution in 2022. The revisions in the number and composition of the clusters over these years could be partly attributed to the changes in the compositions of the value orientations, shifts in the scores respondents gave to each statement in the measures and changes in the demographics of the respondents. Nevertheless, family values, a traditional orientation, and prosocial behaviors are time-tested, consistent and distinctive factors in the clustering of Singaporeans. And despite the revision in the number of clusters over the years, family-oriented clusters still featured prominently in the clustering of Singaporeans.

The four clusters could be typified by four hypothetical individuals: Jasper, the Balancer who values all four orientations similarly; Nathan, the Materialist who has the highest materialism score among the four clusters; May, the Prosocial Family Oriented who values her family and sustainability the most and June, the Traditional Family-Oriented person who values her family and traditions. These personas are intended to serve as archetypes of each of the four clusters and are representative of the unique characteristics that distinguish each group. They are not intended to be ideal clusters or personas for Singaporeans to aspire toward.

The four clusters of Singaporeans in the 2022 QOL Survey differed in their cognitive wellbeing and affective wellbeing, as well as economic wellbeing. The Balancers were the most satisfied with life among the four clusters, while the Materialists were relatively less satisfied. The Pro-Social Family-Oriented members consistently stood out as the segment with the best affective wellbeing. The Pro-Social Family-Oriented Singaporeans were also most satisfied with their economic wellbeing while the Materialists were consistently among the least satisfied clusters. However, as far as trusting other individuals are concerned, regardless of which cluster they belong to, Singaporeans are generally skeptical of others similar to what we have found in the previous 2016 QOL Survey. Almost every cluster in 2022 disagreed that people can be trusted and that people would be fair and try to be helpful.

Rights, politics and wellbeing

While some small changes in rankings were observed for the respondents' satisfaction with certain democratic rights, the 2022 QOL Survey results reflected a decrease in the level of satisfaction for all six democratic rights from 2011. For the past 11 years, the rights to freedom of speech and to criticize the government have been ranked 5th and 6th. If the government and policy makers are concerned about the poor satisfaction levels for the rights to freedom of speech and to criticize the government, more has to be done to improve citizens' access to opportunities and spaces to exercise these two related rights. For younger voters, online activism and advocacy might be one possible avenue as they relied more heavily on online than offline political participation, as noted in Chapter 7.

Generally, many Singaporeans felt they have a duty to vote as voting is compulsory in Singapore and this had a positive effect on Singaporeans' wellbeing, which was also enhanced when they perceived that they have the power to influence government policy or actions. Our results imply that broader and more systemic changes are needed to enhance the internal and external political efficacy of Singaporeans so that they can have a better understanding of and involvement in the political system in addition to voting. As noted in Chapter 7, there are some segments of dissatisfied Singaporeans who would like to see more accountability, transparency and political freedom. As the results varied for different segments of Singaporeans, more in-depth research would be helpful to determine specific concerns and to implement initiatives for better engagement with citizens.

Impact of the COVID-19 pandemic

In Chapter 8, we explored the impact of COVID-19 on Singaporeans' wellbeing in terms of economic impact, health risks, familial factors and social disruptions. The 2022 QOL Survey showed that health risks weighed most heavily on the minds of Singaporeans, followed by job security. Familial disruptions arising partly due to the changes in living arrangements caused by COVID-19 impacted Singaporeans the least. Our detailed analyses and discussion in Chapter 8 have highlighted the complex variations of the impact of the pandemic on particular segments of Singaporeans. While education and income seemed to be positively associated with wellbeing outcomes in the earlier chapters, this was not the case for the impact of the pandemic. In fact, respondents who were more educated and had higher incomes were more adversely affected in some areas. Singaporeans with low education and those with high education appeared to be equally affected by complications arising from domestic family arrangements and domestic violence, compared to those with medium education. Singaporeans with high education and household incomes were also most unhappy about the loss and restriction of activities that they enjoyed, and the most affected by lack of work–life balance.

On 8 March 2023, the Prime Minister's Office released a 92-page White Paper titled "Singapore's Response to COVID-19: Lessons for the Next Pandemic" (Prime Minister's Office Singapore, 2023). This documents has generated a robust debate on the lessons learned, what was done well and what could be improved. It listed eight items that Singapore managed well: (1) the expansion of healthcare capacity (e.g., swabbing and testing operations); (2) successful procurement of COVID-19 vaccination and the high vaccination rate; (3) the successful procurement of food and critical medical supplies; (4) the provision of loans and rebates to businesses; (5) financial support for the vulnerable; (6) the continuation of education through home-based learning; (7) maintenance of high public trust through Multi-Ministry Task Force press conferences and (8) rallying the nation through the SGUnited initiative.

The White Paper also noted six areas of improvement: (1) the outbreak in migrant worker dormitories could have been avoided had early ground surveillance on migrant workers' health and housing been conducted; (2) the number of imported COVID-19 cases could have been reduced if borders were closed more decisively; (3) the mask-wearing policy should have been less definitive in the early days as clinical evidence was evolving; (4) TraceTogether should have been adopted faster at the start for more effective contact tracing; (5) Safe Management Measures could have been simplified and made more flexible and (6) the transition to endemicity could have been calibrated better (Chua, 2023).

The key lessons learnt and proposed initiatives in this White Paper highlighted the commitment of the government to steer the nation of Singapore through the murky waters of the postpandemic world. As noted in our 2022 QOL Survey results, Singaporeans did have a relatively high level of trust in the government and fellow citizens for the journey ahead. However, it looks like more work would need to be done to improve the generalized trust of Singaporeans, as shown in the findings for the clustering of Singaporeans. It is thus important that Singaporeans at all levels of society continue to develop and deepen the trust among the individuals and communities who live and work in Singapore.

Future research directives

This book is part of our continuing efforts to measure the happiness and wellbeing of Singaporeans through the years. There are now at least five nationally representative datasets (survey data collected in 1996, 2001, 2011, 2016 and 2022) over 20 years for satisfaction with life, satisfaction with life domains, personal values and value orientations. For indicators of happiness, enjoyment, achievement and satisfaction with rights, there are four nationally representative datasets (the 2006 AsiaBarometer Survey, the 2011 QOL Survey, the 2016 QOL Survey and the 2022 QOL Survey). Data on satisfaction with democratic rights and views about politics have also been captured for the 2011 QOL Survey, the 2016 QOL Survey and the 2022 QOL Survey. These datasets provide the opportunities for researchers and policy makers to keep track of changes in the wellbeing outcomes over time and to consider ways in which the wellbeing of Singaporeans may have evolved due to changing economic, social and cultural circumstances in Singapore. Future research directives would have to take into account the types of wellbeing measures, the research approaches or techniques used and the subpopulations to be studied.

In terms of wellbeing measures, we have constantly evaluated and experimented with different conceptualizations and scales so that the QOL Surveys stay relevant for the times. For future QOL Surveys, we will continue to refine the measures currently used and introduce measures to account for new developments in the research on wellbeing and changes in the context of Singapore. We had previously expressed (Tambyah & Tan, 2018) that it might be good for Singapore to have an index of the QOL and wellbeing for Singaporeans that would be sustained by government or corporate funding and research support. Ideally, this index would also be accessible for everyday Singaporeans to assess their own wellbeing and it could be made available on an online platform similar to the OECD Better Life Index (Organisation for Economic Co-operation and Development, n.d.). To date, there is still no such index, although researchers in Singapore's universities (e.g., National University of Singapore, the Singapore University of Social Sciences) and research institutes (e.g., the Institute of Policy Studies) have independently conducted studies on the wellbeing of Singaporeans and various key socio-political issues.

The 2022 QOL Survey, like its two predecessors (2011 and 2016) involved the use of cross-sectional surveys to examine important input variables and their influence on wellbeing. Using representative samples of Singaporeans citizens, these surveys conducted at regular intervals (e.g., about every five years) allow us to take snap-shots of Singaporean society, and to assess the extent of change over time. Cross-sectional surveys have built-in corrections for the changing composition of a sampling unit which does not require keeping track of specific individuals over time. However, if possible, it would also be good to have the funding and institutional backing to curate and maintain a nationally representative panel of Singaporeans who would be tracked longitudinally for wellbeing research. Findings from this panel could then be compared with those of cross-sectional sequential studies for greater insights into the wellbeing of Singaporeans, particularly in examining the presence of cohort effects.

While cross-sectional surveys with nationally representative samples provide a bird's-eye view on the wellbeing of Singaporeans, they can be supplemented with other research techniques to focus on certain issues or subpopulations. For example, instead of relying on recall for perceptual measures, one possibility would be to use experience sampling or journaling to study wellbeing. Respondents could be asked to report their wellbeing daily or weekly, and reflect on the reasons for their affective states. While these approaches may be effort intensive, they allow researchers to garner deeper insights into more immediate antecedents, drivers and fluctuations related to wellbeing.

Future studies could also focus on subsets of the Singapore population that are typically underrepresented in national studies. For instance, in the 2022 QOL Survey, we were unable to make comparisons among the different ethnicities due to the small sample sizes of other ethnic groups apart from the Singaporean Chinese respondents. A deeper understanding of the ethnic differences in wellbeing (if any) would allow researchers and policymakers to formulate more targeted policies at improving the wellbeing of Singaporeans. With almost one in four Singaporeans estimated to be 65 years old or above by 2030 (Chin, 2022), there is also a pressing need for in-depth subpopulation studies on the wellbeing of older Singaporeans.

Concluding remarks

Singapore has had its share of challenges and triumphs in 2022 when the QOL Survey was conducted. Despite the economic inse-curities and turmoil brought about by the COVID-19 pandemic and geopolitical tensions, Singapore seemed to be holding up relatively well in terms of economic prosperity with a high per capita GDP and a good standard of living. However, there were Singaporeans who were concerned about their economic well-being, especially those who are not so well educated or with lower household incomes. On the social front, the bonds of family, friends and community are still strong as evidenced by the sat-isfaction levels related to such relationships and the emphasis on family values.

While results of the 2022 QOL Survey painted a gloomy picture of declining wellbeing among Singaporeans, there are some bigger takeaways that we hope readers could glean from this book. One key point to note, among many others, is that while there are some established routes to improve one's life satisfaction or affective wellbeing, there is also room for many different pathways to happiness. Some people may relish the benefits of having a high income, while others are satisfied with their lives through helping others (e.g., May, the Prosocial Family-Oriented archetype). Temporally, an individual can also experience changes in wellbeing across time depending on many factors (e.g., life cycle stage). By understanding what truly makes us happy, all of us can cultivate and integrate positive mindsets and practices in our daily lives that enhance our wellbeing.

As noted by Buettner (2010), Singapore appears to be one of the happiest places to live in, with an economically viable and safe society, family relationships and spiritual groundedness. As Singapore emerges into a postpandemic world, what are some aspirations for the future? We hope that Singaporeans will nurture the right mix of values, trust, openness and democratic processes that would provide common ground for making Singapore a happy and fulfilled society. As always, the pledge is a good reminder to reflect on what binds Singaporeans together as we work toward "happiness, prosperity and progress for our nation".

References

Buettner, D. (2010). *Thrive: Finding happiness in the blue zone's way.* Washington DC: National Geographic.

Chin, S. F. (2022). "S'pore's population ageing rapidly: Nearly 1 in 5 citizens is 65 years and older". The Straits Times. www.straitstimes.com/singapore/singapores-population-ageing-rapidly-184-of-citizens-are-65-years-and-older

Chua, N. (2023, 20 March). *7 in 10 S'pore residents in good shape postpandemic; youth, caregivers see drop in quality of life: Poll.* The Straits Times. Retrieved 1 May 2023, from www.straitstimes.com/singapore/7-in-10-s-pore-residents-emerged-from-covid-19-in-good-shape-but-a-higher-proportion-of-youth-report-drop-in-quality-of-life-survey

Ministry of Health Singapore. (2022). "Report on excess mortality during the COVID-19 pandemic up to June 2022". Retrieved 29 April 2023 from www.moh.gov.sg/docs/librariesprovider5/resources-statistics/reports/report-on-excess-mortality-during-the-covid-pandemic-18sep2022.pdf

Ministry of Health Singapore. (2023). "Living life to the fullest: 2023 action plan for successful ageing". Retrieved 1 May 2023, from www.moh.gov.sg/docs/librariesprovider3/action-plan/2023-action-plan.pdf.

Ministry of Social and Family Development Singapore. (2022). *White paper on Singapore's women development: Towards a fairer and more inclusive society*. Retrieved 1 May 2023 from www.scwo.org.sg/wp-content/uploads/2022/03/White-Paper-on-Singapore-Womens-Development.pdf.

Ng, K. G. (2023, 7 February). *"Be careful what you wish for": Lively debate on keeping public housing affordable and accessible*. The Straits Times. Retrieved 1 May 2023, from www.straitstimes.com/singapore/politics/be-careful-what-you-wish-for-lively-debate-on-keeping-public-housing-affordable-and-accessible

Organisation for Economic Co-operation and Development. (n.d.). *How's life?* OECD Better Life Index. Retrieved 1 May 2023, from www.oecdbetterlifeindex.org/

Prime Minister's Office Singapore. (2023). *White paper on Singapore's response to COVID-19: Lessons for the next pandemic*. Retrieved 1 May 2023, from www.gov.sg/docs/default-source/media/gov/covid-19-white-paper/publication/white_paper_on_singapore_response_to_covid19_130323.pdf?sfvrsn=c33ec046_1.

Tambyah, S. K., & Tan, S. J. (2013). *Happiness and wellbeing: The Singaporean experience*. London: Routledge.

Tambyah, S. K., & Tan, S. J. (2018). *Happiness, wellbeing and society: What matters for Singaporeans*. London: Routledge.

The Workers' Party. (2022, 13 September). *Adjournment motion: Ensuring the housing needs of singles and Singaporeans are met – speech by Louis Chua*. Retrieved 1 May 2023, from www.wp.sg/adjournment-motion-ensuring-the-housing-needs-of-singles-and-singaporeans-are-met-speech-by-louis-chua/

United Nations Development Programme. (2022). *Human development report 2021/2022 uncertain times, unsettled lives: Shaping our future in a transforming world*. Retrieved 1 May 2023, from https://hdr.undp.org/system/files/documents/global-report-document/hdr2021-22pdf_1.pdf.

Zachariah, N. A. (2023, 21 April). *The gist: PM Lee calls for unity amid challenges as MPs debate housing affordability, help for singles*. The Straits Times. Retrieved 1 May 2023, from www.straitstimes.com/singapore/the-gist-pm-lee-calls-for-unity-amid-challenges-as-mps-debate-housing-affordability-help-for-singles

Index